Praise for Malcolm McClean and *Bear Hunt*

'… *Bear Hunt* shows everyone that everything we do counts and that if you have passion, you can move mountains.'

Michael Lynch AM
Chief Executive, South Bank Centre
Formerly Chief Executive, Sydney Opera House

'What a world it would be if more of us could earn our living doing what we love. *Bear Hunt* provides a formula which will inspire and challenge you by giving insights into the things they don't teach you at school – but should. *Bear Hunt* should be available on prescription.'

Baroness Cumberlege of Newick
Parliamentary Under-Secretary of State for Health 1992–97

'Malcolm McClean's work is an inspiration – simple, effective and clear. For anyone who ever wanted to change their work and their life, this book will get you on track. Malcolm McClean has "original thinker" written on his face. If he says something, believe him – it works.'

Kate Marlow
Presenter, Channel 4's Reality Check

'I've been lucky enough to earn my living doing what I love. *Bear Hunt* offers a route for others to do the same.'

Sir Bobby Charlton

'I shudder to think what might have been had my post-graduate applications to the Post Office or the Inland Revenue been successful. I am doubly blessed that my career, being amply paid for doing what I love, wasn't really intended. How refreshing that Malcolm McClean offers a more structured path towards such rewards.'

Alan Green
Football commentator, BBC Radio Five Live

Bear Hunt

Bear Hunt

Earn your living by doing what you love

Malcolm McClean

CAPSTONE

Published in 2005 by Capstone Publishing Limited (a Wiley Company), The Atrium, Southern Gate
Chichester, West Sussex, PO19 8SQ, England
Phone (+44) 1243 779777

Email (for orders and customer service enquires): cs-books@wiley.co.uk
Visit our Home Page on www.wiley.co.uk or www.wiley.com

Other Wiley Editorial Offices

John Wiley & Sons, Inc. 111 River Street, Hoboken, NJ 07030, USA
Jossey-Bass, 989 Market Street, San Francisco, CA 94103-1741, USA
Wiley-VCH Verlag GmbH, Pappellaee 3, D-69469 Weinheim, Germany
John Wiley & Sons Australia Ltd, 42 McDougall Street, Milton, Queensland 4064, Australia
John Wiley & Sons (Asia) Pte Ltd, 2 Clementi Loop #02-01, Jin Xing Distripark, Singapore 129809
John Wiley & Sons Canada Ltd, 22 Worcester Road, Etobicoke, Ontario, Canada, M9W 1L1

Wiley also publishes its books in a variety of electronic formats. Some content that appears in print may not be available in electronic books.

Library of Congress Cataloging-in-Publication Data is available

British Library Cataloguing in Publication Data

A catalogue record for this book is available from the British Library

ISBN-10: 1841126667 (PB); ISBN-13: 978-1-84112-666-1 (PB)

Typeset in Palatino by Sparks Computer Solutions Ltd, Oxford (www.sparks.co.uk)
Printed and bound in Great Britain by TJ International Ltd, Padstow, Cornwall
This book is printed on acid-free paper responsibly manufactured from sustainable forestry in which at least two trees are planted for each one used for paper production.
10 9 8 7 6 5 4 3 2

To
Leanne, Hollie and Callum

You are what you believe you are

Contents

1 How to earn your living by doing what you love   1

2 Love Saves The Day – how to rediscover your passions   11

3 You are what you believe – how imagery can transform your life   25

4 The sticky ball principle and the power of connection   37

5 Luck be a lady tonight – applying the science of luck   61

6 Develop your millionaire mind   77

7 Think like an eight-year-old   103

8 Does van Nistelrooy slouch? Learn to get yourself into the zone   121

9 Change your world – how small things make a big difference   139

10 Aha, ker-ching   147

Notes and references   153

Index   155

1

How to earn your living by doing what you love

You can make a choice. We all have the power to make choices. Yet, when it comes to the way we earn our living, so many of us make choices that are disempowering, make us miserable and drain us. So much so, that it seems that only a lucky few people can say that they earn their living by doing what they love.

These people are in fact no luckier than you have the capability to be. Neither are there as few of them as you might imagine.

The truly great news is that these people are finding the clues that will enable you to live a life that you can love and earn your living from it – if you have the courage, conviction and belief.

More and more people suffer from what could be called 'Sunday Evening Syndrome': they look ahead to another working week and ask 'Is this it? Is this all there is?' Research figures continue to confirm that we've never had more material wealth yet we've never felt more dissatisfied. One recent survey showed that only 10% of people regard themselves as 'happy'.

Stress-related illness is rife: throwing a 'sickie' is the most common reason for missing work. Holidays have become an essential survival tactic, yet for many people only provide a temporary antidote to ward off their feelings of dissatisfaction with their lives.

Our lust for escapism and dreams of a better life fail to address the real issue: work drains us. Earning a living is seen as the hard stuff – an essential activity that lacks joy. Work is something that takes us away from the things we would rather be doing. Most people are just not earning their living by doing what they love.

In fact, love and work are rarely mentioned in the same breath. They are considered as two elements of life that are mutually exclusive. Yet think about it: love is something that most of us intuitively understand and believe we deserve. Love can make the spirits soar and the heart race, yet it can be frustrating, difficult and elusive. Nevertheless we need it to make sense of life. It makes us feel whole.

Work? Well, work is something else. We know we have to do it but we don't immediately associate passion and lust with our work. Particularly in Britain, we spend more time working than being with the ones we love. Long hours workers (those that work more than 48 hours a week) are more prevalent than in other European countries, where 11% work long hours, compared with 22% here.

So often the result is that we become miserable and increasingly stressed. Studies have found that working long hours is associated with a range of negative effects, such as decreased productivity, poor performance, health problems and lower employee motivation. In turn, this inevitably leads to us paying even less attention to the people we care about the most.

The outcome? A loveless life. Is it any wonder that so many of us are unhappy?

We all deserve happiness. We have a right to love what we do, and we can choose. Happiness, apart from being a state we all desire, is actually good for us: researchers in Holland have found that 'happy' people live on average nine years longer and suffer less from heart disease or other illnesses.

So why don't people just go ahead and do what they love?

Some, I'm sure, feel trapped. Trapped by the comfortable existence that they have established; their salary; their benefits; their status; other people's expectations; their responsibilities; the house; the mortgage; the children; and so the list could go on.

Others lack belief. We are what we believe. If we don't believe in ourselves, how can we expect anyone else to?

Others still are simply under a misapprehension. They believe that doing what you love requires a massive amount of cash to invest, some technical knowledge of business and financial mumbo-jumbo or is downshifting. They create a mistaken belief that because you are doing something that you love, you will have to abandon any notion of success and accept less money.

I want to blow away these barriers and myths. You need not feel trapped. I want to show you how to look at things in a different way: you can create and realize new beliefs that will transform your life and you don't necessarily have to be a technical or financial whizz-kid to live a life that you can love.

What's more, I have proven that you can, if you want to, earn more by doing what you love. It does not have to mean living a subsistence lifestyle.

Think about it: so many people earn a good living and have comfortable lifestyles simply by doing something they hate. Why can't you earn a great living doing something that you think is great? When you invest your energy, passion and love towards something that matters, their effects become magnified.

Yet money alone does not buy happiness. You will see from many of the case studies in this book that for those who do what they love, money is secondary – in some cases, not even an issue.

Through their stories and my own experiences, I will be introducing a series of principles that, taken together, provide the formula for earning your living by doing what you love. It is not a rigid blueprint that will work in exactly the same way with all people at all times. It should be treated more like a recipe. You should decide which ingredients are most suited to your tastes, your situation and your desire. You should play around with them to find out which works best for you. Most of all, you will have to put in the most important ingredient – you.

All of you: your passion, desire, courage, determination, vision, creativity, tenacity, resilience and of course your love. If you can do this, in time, your life can be transformed.

You may ask how I came by this formula. You may wonder how I can say with absolute conviction that it works. You may be concerned if it is temporary or lasting, or you may think it is highly personal and not learnable.

Before I introduce people who are just like me – people from all walks of life who do what they love – let me address these issues.

Great things with great people

Every day for the last five years, I can say that I have earned my living by doing what I love. Sure, there have been ups and downs; trials and tribulations; mistakes and misjudgements; times when I have had to put duty before enjoyment; and amongst this has been a tremendous feeling of intellectual and professional fulfilment, success, reward, freedom, laughter, and contribution. As an added bonus, every now and then, I do something for free that makes me feel proud. Just because I want to, and there is nobody to tell me that I can't.

I'm able to do this not because I enjoyed privilege. I was raised in one of Britain's most deprived neighbourhoods. It's not because I am educated in the traditional sense – I went to a sink school and left at 16. And it's not because I am free from commitments. I have three dependent children, two mortgages and nobody to depend upon for a living except myself.

I am able to do this because I began with belief and along the way added the other ingredients of the formula:

- passion;
- imagery;
- thinking like an eight-year-old;
- working in the zone;
- the sticky ball principle and the power of connections;
- modelling entrepreneurs;
- cultivating luck; and
- noticing that small things can have big effects.

You will notice that I have not included the term 'write a business plan'. Funnily enough, not one of the case studies in this book referred to this either. That's not to say that it may not be important to you at some stage in your development; it just appears that in doing what you love, the essence of it seems to be 'concentrate on what's important – the rest will look after itself'.

The way I found out what it was that I loved doing is in itself a lesson, but perhaps wasn't the ideal way to do it. I left it until I was in crisis, as so many people do. They wait until they are made redundant, or there is a death in the family, or they suffer ill health. They postpone happiness, waiting for the next pay rise, the next promotion or even retirement, believing that then they will have the time and space to be happy. Life is rarely that tidy and often people who postpone happiness never actually get there.

I suppose if I am honest, I was one of these people. I almost saw disaster coming, but I was a little too late to change it.

Over the years, through a series of chance occurrences and a little bit of serendipity, I had emerged as a partner in a successful management consultancy. Along with two colleagues, we created it and expanded it and we were proud of it. Yet it became a monster.

I would travel 60,000 miles a year. Without noticing, I had become a workaholic, working 60, 70, 80, sometimes 100 hours a week. On some occassions I had completed a normal working week by Wednesday lunchtime. My wife, who was keeping a young family together, was soon to become my ex-wife.

Realizing that I had fallen out of love with this life, and that I was totally drained and burned out, I decided to end my association with the business. So with no job, an impending divorce and no home at this stage, I wondered what I would do. I had a few hazy ideas, of course – I would have been a fool not to have. Now I needed a purpose and I needed it rather quickly.

I talked incessantly to myself about what it was that I wanted to do. I replayed in my mind past successes, times when I had felt really alive, I thought about the constraints that organizations and institutions can place upon us. And then, one evening, it came to me. I said it out loud to see how it felt. I said,

'I just want to do great things with great people.' There was nobody there to hear it, but it just felt right to me. So I wrote it down.

I began to create images in my head about what this idea might look like, and over the years I have replayed these mental pictures many times, as well as the image of my coming up with and enunciating what I wanted to do.

Some years later I had a chance meeting with Dr Gerry Epstein, probably the world's leading authority on the use of mental imagery. Until then, I had not realized the significance of this simple act of replaying an image in the mind. This is something we will cover later when I introduce Gerry as a case study.

So that was how it began: not with a complex business plan, but by rediscovering what I was passionate about. I then had to bring into play all the other elements of the formula.

Elements that I have since observed, in one form or another, in a wide range of people that earn their living by doing what they love.

Great people doing great things.

I have a total conviction that the formula that I am going to unfold to you in this book works. Partly because I have been able for the last five years to wander around, read a lot, talk to interesting people, mess about with ideas, write sometimes, speak sometimes and sell ideas, advice and knowledge. In short, I continue to do great things with great people. Who would ever have thought that you could make a great living just by doing that?

The other part of my conviction comes from the people that have come into my life since I have been doing this. Some have become friends, colleagues, partners or collaborators. Others I have met simply because of seemingly chance occurrences whilst I was thinking about this book.

These are some of the great people doing great things whose stories and observations will begin to unfold the formula:

- **Andrew Mawson OBE** is an irreverent reverend. He behaves more like Richard Branson than a man of the cloth. He was destined for a life as a telecoms engineer, which to his father's delight meant a good salary, holidays and a pension. But Andrew wanted answers to the 'why?' questions. He wanted to make a difference, yet he wanted to do it in an entrepreneurial way.

   Anyone going to Bromley by Bow in East London will see that he has: once Britain's most run-down neighbourhood, it is now admired across the world for its pioneering approach to developing communities.
- **Sandra Deeble** wrote a story when she was eight years old and received her first rejection letter from *Twinkle* comic. She never wrote

another thing until at the age of 32 she followed her intuition, after years of going against it.

She is now a successful writer for a range of quality newspapers and magazines, has written five books for a publishing house, and is writing her first novel. She has no journalistic qualifications whatsoever and she has never had a business plan. Her whole world changed after a remarkable experience which she describes as not a 'head thing'. She lives the life that she has dreamed of since she was eight.

- By contrast, **Robert Swan** refused to let go of his childhood dream. He grew up with an unshakeable belief that he would make it happen. It all started when as a young boy he became captivated whilst watching actor John Mills in the film *Scott of the Antarctic*. He knew then what he wanted to do with his life.

  Not for Swan, a career as an actor. He was determined that he would follow in Scott's footsteps and walk to the South Pole.

  Against all the odds – physical, financial, logistical – he did. Later he became the first man in history to walk to both poles. His next job is even bigger – to save Antarctica.

- With a successful psychiatric practice in New York, **Dr Gerry Epstein** enjoyed a comfortable and successful life. Then a chance meeting with an Algerian lady in Jerusalem opened up a new path. It was a difficult path that caused him to be ostracized by his professional colleagues: he began to develop the techniques of mental imagery, or 'waking dream' therapy, that had no place in the Freudian tradition.

  His commitment and passion drove him through some difficult times. He is now highly respected and sought-after as one of the world's leading authorities on mental imagery.

- Staring down the barrel of a shotgun, onetime vendor of professional muscle and intimidation **Greg Davis** decided that his life, if he was to continue to have one, had to change.

  Having had a tough upbringing, he was passionate about the potential that lies in young people on our most run-down estates. He started with nothing and has created something on an estate renowned for shooting, stabbing and drug-dealing. He has plans to do much more.

- **Eugenie Harvey** grew up in Australia. As long as she can remember, she has always had a feeling in the pit of her stomach that she would do something interesting one day. Something special.

  She had a mixed blessing. She was remarkably good at public relations, something she hated. She came to London to re-invent herself, yet she found herself at 'rock bottom', at her lowest ebb, before she had what she calls her 'ker-ching' moment.

When you are down, they say, 'it is not how far you fall, it is how high you bounce'. She has bounced. She now loves what she does, and it is something quite special. She spearheads a movement called We Are What We Do – its mission is to change the world. Its first publication, *Change the World for a Fiver*, sold 100,000 copies in its first three months and spawned a TV animation series.

- In the City of London, merchant bankers can earn £250,000 per year. **Phillip Collins** was one of them. Yet even this mega-salary was not enough to fill the void that he felt inside himself. Something was missing.

  It was passion, a feeling of doing something worth doing, and in the end this proved stronger than the lure of the cash. He walked away, not knowing what he was going to do with his life. He has emerged as the director of an influential think tank and he loves what he does – even though he's about £200,000 a year worse off.

- *Picture Book*, *Men and Women* and *A New Flame* were the first three albums released by rock band Simply Red. When the band spent a year in Italy recording an album, drummer **Chris Joyce** fell in love with the food and the wine.

  When the time came to hang up his drumsticks, his first instinct was to invest in a recording studio and his own record label. After a lot of money had gone down the tubes, he realized something – he loved music, but he hated the music business. He created a new concept: a café that thinks it's a shop that thinks it's a deli. His accountants couldn't understand it and told him he was crazy.

  He calls his place Love Saves The Day and it has. After four years of nurturing, experimentation and mistakes, he now takes a salary from it and has great new plans.

All of the people featured in this book can provide you with the clues to a life that you can love. They will inspire you, move you and amuse you. These are not *special* people – they are ordinary people who have chosen to lead extraordinary lives.

Who is this book for?

It's for anybody. Anybody that is miserable in their work; is underachieving; who wants to use their talents to the full; is about to return to employment after a break; is about to retire and wants to do something; is unemployed; is successful but wants another challenge; is about to leave full-time education and enter the world of work. In particular:

- **Public sector workers driven by targets.** I often hear teachers saying that they signed up in order to be educators, or doctors and nurses complaining that they seem to spend less and less time doing what they love – caring for patients. The whole of the public sector has become subjected to ever more inspection, testing and target-setting and, as a result, a lot more administration and bureaucracy.
- **Commuters.** The daily commute is getting longer as pressure on the roads and the public transport system grows. It's crowded, unpleasant and tiring, and it consumes an awful lot of your life. People are commuting further and working longer. No wonder they are too exhausted to have much of a family life.
- **Underachievers.** You might think you are special. The chances are, if you think you are, you probably are. Many people never quite fulfil their immense potential: sometimes through accident of birth, or because they were too busy caring for others, or because of relationships – all sorts of reasons. It's OK to be a late developer. Or would you rather have it in the back of you mind for the rest of your life that you never did quite what you would have loved, and you never truly realized your immense potential?
- **Silver surfers.** The art of growing old is to die young – but as late as possible. People are living longer and often retiring younger. For many of those who have worked for a lifetime, retirement could last for 30 or 40 years. That's a long time to prune roses. Many people now think about doing something they can love.
- **The unemployed.** Just because you are unemployed does not mean you don't have a value. We all have special talents, and some of this county's most successful people have spent time on the dole. You are what you believe you are and, if you want to, you can earn a living doing what you love.
- **Gap-year students.** University was great and you are still in touch with all your friends. Then to top it all you spent a year travelling the world, meeting new people. Now you are in your office and this is reality. Nobody told you it would be like this. It probably will, but only for 40 years or so.
- **Mums.** For some years now you've put everyone else first. With the kids at school, it's time to think about you and what you want. Endless coffee mornings, perhaps? You could go back to your old career if you had one. Or you could think about doing something you love.

- **The mid-life crisis/success.** Funny things happen when you reach middle age. For many, it is a crisis: 'there's the half-time whistle – what have I done?' For others it's a time to take stock. You may have been successful in your career and want a new challenge or you may have sold a business. Just because you have money, it doesn't guarantee future success or happiness, as some of the case studies in this book have proven.
- **Dormant enterprisers.** You've always wanted to work for yourself, but with one thing or another, the time has never been quite right. Do you know what? The time will never be exactly 'right'. Use this book to get your head right and the rest will follow.

Anyone can read this book, but only the courageous will act. I can't give you the courage, but I can give you a whole raft of tips, tools, techniques and stories from other people who have had the courage to change their lives. I hope it will inspire you to summon your own reserves of courage.

How to get the best from this book

This book brings together a whole series of themes that will set you towards a life that you can love and sustain you during the downs as well as the ups. It won't tell you what you should do on Monday, Tuesday or Friday. You are going to have to do a lot of figuring out for yourself, depending on your context, circumstances and what precisely you are aiming to do.

To get the best from this book, you must keep an open mind. There will be things in here that will surprise you, that you may think are outlandish or even just so simple that they seem beyond belief. Engage with the ideas, play with the thoughts, test, experiment and be persistent – sometimes things don't always go right first time.

Take heart and inspiration from the people featured in this book. Their stories are here to help you develop your own insights, to allow you to learn from their mistakes and their successes, and to show you that all the ideas in this book are not just academic theories – people are using them. They are earning a living by doing what they love. Are you?

There is nothing about these people that could lead you to say 'well it's all right for them, they had it easy.' All of them made choices about their lives. Some of those choices were very hard to make. Others were courageous. Many have had their sanity called into question. Yet, in the final analysis, these people have had the courage of their convictions and set out on a path that suits them.

Each of them in their own right is achieving things that make them feel good about the work that they do.

Across all of them – their different backgrounds, circumstances, passions and beliefs – some common themes emerge: the elements of what I call the formula. Some stories highlight only one element, others mix several together.

The exciting thing is that they are all elements that are learnable to some degree, and over the coming chapters I will break them down so that you can choose to follow the elements that are useful to you.

You are in the same position as I am, and all the case studies in the book are, regarding your future and the life you want to live.

You have a choice. You can choose. The only limits are the limits that you place upon yourself. You are what you believe you are.

If you believe that you are destined for a life that you can love, then choose. Choose to come with us on this journey. A journey that will unfold a most remarkable and unlikely formula.

A small thing that can have a big effect.

2

Love Saves The Day –
how to rediscover your passions

The young Mick Hucknall was just a kid from Manchester. But he had a voice. It was to become the voice of pop group Simply Red.

It is a voice that has sold over 40 million albums. In 1982, just before he was launched onto the music scene, he formed a band around him. Drummer Chris Joyce got the call. He toured the world and made three groundbreaking albums: *Picture Book*, *Men and Women*, and *A New Flame*.

Then, to use his words, he 'got sacked'. His first instinct was to plough his money into his own recording studio and his Planet 4 record label. Then, after a while, he realized something. He *loved* music but he *hated* the music business.

Of course, you have to be careful. When you take something that you love and earn your living from it, love can turn sour. Then what are you left with?

You don't have a living, and the thing that you love now has some negative associations.

So, before you give up your job and tear off to your new life, pause a little. Take some time to properly reflect on the nature of love, and then reassess what kind of person you are and what you are really passionate about: you may find that it is not always the thing that you love *most* that is the right thing for you.

If you are like me, you will love many things to varying degrees. You must think carefully if the thing that you pursue fits with the things that give you most pleasure.

Chris Joyce's first love was music, but he had other loves as well.

In 1982 I joined Simply Red and the first European country we went to on tour was Italy. I just had the most amazing time there – I was blown away with the culture. I suppose it was the wine and the food. We were privileged and lucky. I got introduced to loads of food that I'd never seen, never tried.

It changed my palette. It turned out that in 1989 we were looking for somewhere to go and make our third album. We decided to have a year together. We rented some apartments in Galerati, just outside of Milan.

We all loved it. It gave me an opportunity to live there. Nobody spoke English so I had to learn Italian. It was really good to gain that experience and knowledge there.

After an amazingly successful period with the band, he made the decision to try something other than being a hands-on musician.

I've always had stars in my eyes. It was a difficult decision at the time to give up music. I set up a recording business. It drove me mad. I loved music but I didn't like the business of music. I lost a lot of money. I knew it wasn't for me.

So now he had to find something else to do – and it had to be something he loved.

So my life has always been about doing, you know, something that I love, really. I'm stubborn and obstinate in that sort of sense. In a way I've always been my own boss.

In 1995 he had met his wife Becky, who coincidently had also lived for a time in Italy.

It was in 1996 that the bomb went off in Manchester. There was a huge amount of regeneration going on at that stage. We were living in the city centre.

The Italian experience had developed an appreciation of great food and wine in both of us. Seeing all the regeneration and what was going on in Manchester led us to believe that it would be a good idea to have some form of delicatessen in Manchester, because there was nothing along those lines. You've got the Jewish delis outside the centre, but people were beginning to move into the city centre with no provision.

People were paying a fortune for city apartments and a Spar outside the centre was the kind of nearest shop.

So you're spending £150,000–£200,000 on an apartment and all you have is a Spar, or you get into the car and drive out somewhere to a Sainsbury's.

We just thought that there was an opportunity there. It was actually 1999 when we opened the doors, but we spent two years previous to that doing research. First of all we started with a blank canvas. I'd been a musician and that was it. I basically had a passion for food and wine.

From the blank canvas emerged Love Saves The Day. An apt title for somebody who has always had to do what he loves. It is part café, part deli, part 'theatre'.

We were setting out the concept, which was very vague when we first started. We were looking at an urban convenience store. That was the idea behind it and in some ways we have turned out to be like that, we kind of just had to find the right balance between bums on seats and what we had on the shelves.

We rebuilt the shelving and made the deli side of it the 'theatre', the ambience of coming into Love Saves The Day. People seem to really like that – the shop aspect going on around the café and restaurant appeals to people a lot – and the concept is that basically anything on the menu is what people can buy to take out. Ready meals for a city centre urban crowd.

It was the name that caught my eye originally as I headed for a meeting in Manchester one day, and that is how I came to meet Chris.

The name came about because Becky's sister came on board with her partner. It was something about the kind of family unit that we are that appealed very much. And in my kind of subversive way, I liked the way that we could abbreviate it to LSD.

There are lots of ideas you could use for graphics, marketing. We haven't used the LSD thing very much yet.

We kind of used it as the working name and then had doubts: 'Should we call it The Smithfield Deli or something safe?' Then we just thought we would be crazy. The name is fantastic. It's one of those names that people either love or hate. People call up and you answer the phone saying 'Love Saves The Day' – and you get all sorts of replies, like 'Oh, does it?'

Others say what a really beautiful name. Immediately it gets a reaction. Being based here on Tib Street, in one of Manchester's sleazier districts, some people came in looking for porn.

We decided to stick with the name.

Being new to business, Chris sought advice. In the end he chose to back his own instincts.

I saw various accountants and they couldn't get their head round it. It wasn't this and it wasn't that, it was this kind of mix of uses. It was a new kind of model of a store of this style. People have compared us to New York delis and I've spent a lot of time in New York. I've just been there on a research trip and it wouldn't be out of place if we opened a Love Saves The Day in New York.

The accountants were all very negative about it. It's when you get so far down the line with something, there's no pulling back no matter what advice people give you. You just think, 'We had our instincts of how we wanted to carry on.'

I've always been a bit of a risk taker – Becky's more on the cautious side but has got used to the risk element. When I go for something I go for it and that is it. It's a very blinkered vision.

The whole team were so passionate about this that they were prepared to ride through any storm.

The first four years were extremely difficult, because we didn't know what we were doing. It was passion that drove us for those first four years, because it certainly wasn't bloody money. It cost me money for those first four years.

We had a lot of stress: we set up a business, had a baby, moved house, all in the same year. I had to give personal guarantees.

Only in this last two years have we got better with our accounting. I'd been a musician, not a businessman, then I had to learn the art of business. Now we have people around us who bring other skills. We changed our accountant, and we have turned the business around.

Becky and I weren't taking any money out for four years. Our advisor told us, 'You are f****** crazy. You haven't got a business, it's a charity.' She gave us a bollocking and we got our act together.

14

We are good with people but we are not tough – that's why we needed other people on board. We've got better. We have a tighter ship now.

I saw a business opportunity and it came together by getting the right people around me. In those first years it was hard, but we used to get such positive feedback from people that it seemed worthwhile carrying on.

There were times when I would have packed it in and I wasn't getting any money out of it. My house was re-mortgaged. The city was developing at a pace and it always gave me heart that we had something good. People kept coming in saying we should open one of these shops in Brighton and elsewhere.

There have been times when I would have sold shares to get some money in, but I'm glad that didn't happen because it would have watered down what we were trying to do.

As the business has become established, LSD has become a real hit on the Manchester scene.

This place? It's amazing who comes in here. It's not something that we shout about, but every kind of hip mover or shaker in Manchester is one of our customers during the week.

It reaffirms my belief in what we are doing. What gives me a buzz is seeing the place full and it working well.

Six years later, we are just starting to look at rolling the concept out. Every developer that is doing anything in this city tries to get us to move into their building.

It's interesting how often people who have achieved success go on to look for success in a different sphere. They begin to ask themselves, how can I make a contribution?

The philosophy is that in the long term we would like to set up an LSD for areas that are down at heel, where we would open up a local type of store in poorer areas, where we could run a non-profit-making type of thing and give something back into the community. Create jobs and opportunities.

What we are trying to do is encourage things. Carol is from Moss Side – she started having kids at 16. Her son has been with us since he was 11. She used to bring him in on Saturdays so we got him washing up. He's now enrolled in a college course. I feel heartened he's worked hard and created his own luck. He's going forward in very positive way. He cooks in the kitchen. He's f****** lovin' it. He's got to do a bit more English and maths, but he's got all the skills to cook. He still lives in Moss Side with his mum and still gets stopped by the police, but he's got some confidence in himself now.

Chris Joyce has grappled with something new and overcome all sorts of obstacles because it is in his nature to do what he loves. One might think he is a lucky man, but he has a very clear opinion on that.

You create your own luck. You've got to be out and about and doing things for things to happen. If you are sitting down in your living room, waiting for things to happen, they won't. You've got to create your own luck.

So he has.

Love works

Chris Joyce's story clearly shows that you can do what you love, although love has its ups and downs, and sometimes you have to fight for it. It's the same if you want to love your work.

If you are about to change your life for a life that you can love, it's important that you take a little time to properly understand the nature of love and passion. You need to prepare yourself for what could be a roller coaster ride.

We want to do what we love, so what do we know about love?

Is there really any such thing as love? Well, according to Robert Winston, author of *The Human Mind: And How to Make the Most of It*, 'fortunately the answer is yes'. Yet what is it about this elusive state of mind that we so cherish, and how can we take that feeling and meld it to our work?

Before we try to work out what we love and how we would love to earn our living, let's spend some time trying to understand the nature of love. We will need this understanding, because when we set out to earn our living by doing what we love, it will not always be easy.

You've got to get beyond lust

Scientists have found that there are three separate and distinct phases of the whole experience of falling in love: lust, attraction and attachment. Anthropologist Helen Fisher thinks that each of these stages had a different evolutionary purpose. Lust evolved to get us looking for mates; attraction to help us focus our attentions on an ideal partner; and attachment to stay with them (so that we could raise our offspring).

At first, we experience lust. We all know that feeling in the context of the opposite sex – that yearning or longing for something that we desire. The object of our desire may not be ours, yet somehow, we repeatedly think about it. Sometimes opportunity knocks and we grab it with both hands; at other times, our yearning becomes so great that we feel compelled to take action. Quite often we just lust and yearn, lust and yearn.

All over the world, commuter trains are packed with people who are yearning for a better life. Most of them yearn, then yearn a little more. They never get beyond lust, they never seize opportunity and they never experience that extraordinary compulsion to act. It is a sad fact that many grow old only to yearn for their lost opportunities.

Though we all experience a lot of lust, in the overall scheme of things very little of it gets beyond a fanciful yearning. If we are to earn our living by doing what we love, we must make the object of our desires so compelling that we get hooked on it and take massive sustained action to make it materialize. Just as many of us have done when we have fallen in love with a man or a woman.

In doing so, we move from lust to attraction. Scientists have shown that we experience actual pleasure when we see an attractive face. Such attraction is vital for the continuation of the species. Likewise, we have to experience actual pleasure to do the thing that we love for a living. The feelings we get must not be ignored.

If you are searching for the thing that you might do for a living, but are not sure what you love, think back to the times and the activities when you have felt extraordinary pleasure – a sense of achievement or a feeling of making a contribution. Attraction is really a form of focused attention and goal-oriented behaviour. We move towards something consistently, passionately and fervently in order to get something we long for, whether it be the continuation of the species or the continuation of our work, or the feeling of elation that comes with being around the object of your attraction. It is the feeling, that 'rush', of falling in love.

Feelings of falling in love can seem almost like an obsession – some have said it is akin to an episode of mental illness. People become more irrational about the object of their affection and idealize them. This happens when you find the work that you really want to do. This irrationality, obsession and idealization are important factors in helping you to become determined to overcome the many obstacles you will encounter.

Over time, this first mad, spontaneous fever of love becomes replaced by a more solid partnership. Something more stable. In the case of love, something more suited to raising children; in the case of our work, perhaps something more suited to paying the bills consistently.

Sometimes it's irrational

Some researchers suggest that the relationships that are the most long-lived are those that are able to preserve some of the earlier, less rational, exciting and passionate elements. I believe that people who can maintain the spontaneity and passion in their work, who can be principled and illogical sometimes, will earn their living by doing what they love – for longer.

The 'pink lens effect'

Dr Ellen Berscheld of the University of Minnesota studied what she called the 'pink lens effect'. She found that couples who idealize their partners make over-optimistic judgements about them.

For example, we may think that our lovers are 'brilliant' and wonderful; we may overestimate their intelligence, their generosity, their honesty and even their looks. For most people, this pink lens effect decreases over time; that's when we determine that 'we love them for what they are'.

Some other studies have shown that couples who idealized each other the most were also those who had the longest relationships. So it takes some irrationality to make up a happy marriage or to earn your living doing what you love.

You must accentuate the positive and eliminate the negative. This is a great asset to a relationship and it is a great asset to doing what you love.

The man who lost more shirts than Marks & Spencer – then found out how to work out what you love

Gavin Cargill was at the peak of his profession, but when he went into business for himself he says he lost 'more shirts than Marks & Spencer sold'. Much later, he found out why. The talents that he had used to get to the top of his profession were not ones suited to running a business. He had no talent for business and therefore he had no passion for it.

According to Cargill, people love what they do when they have an opportunity to use their talents every day. The trouble is, most people don't even recognize what their talents are. They might know what their skills are and where their knowledge lies. Many people will say 'I wish I was talented' or 'I don't have any talent'. This is simply not true. Everybody has key talent themes and now there is a way to find out what they are.

Gavin Cargill though, had to find out the hard way.

Most of my working life had been in the area of financial services. There didn't seem to be any other route. I wasn't an academic I had great difficulty in getting myself into subjects that I wasn't interested in.

I got a job as a bank clerk and made my first discovery. If you took out an insurance policy, you became an agent. So they asked me to introduce people that I knew, and gave me the commission.

I started to talk to people I knew – I had a very limited knowledge, but it was sufficient – and I would get the commission. After one year, and at just 20 years of age, I was actually getting nearly twice as much from my commission as I was from my salary as a bank clerk.

I thought, 'Well, that's interesting.' So I asked my agent, how do I do your job? You seem to go around talking to bank managers and accountants telling them stories.

They said I was very young, but they would take a risk, and they carved up a little bit of Fife in Scotland that they never did any business in anyway. They said, 'We could let you loose here. Just do what you do and see what happens.'

They gave him a Morris 1000 and he tried to make himself look older.

Because I was only 20, I had this thing that I had to try and look older. I had these starched collars that detached and an umbrella.

Two years later I had doubled my income. I was a slow learner, but once I understood what I was talking about I loved going out there and talking about it.

By the age of 26, I was number two in the league table of advisers in the whole of the UK. All of a sudden I was successful.

At the time he didn't stop to think about why he was being successful and what it was that he loved. If he had, he might have saved himself a lot of heartache.

Now, though, he can see what it was that he loved.

I enjoyed communicating ideas in ways that people understood. I worked beside people who seemed to love to impress people by their understanding of the complexity of financial planning. I seemed to get a buzz from saying 'Look at this' in a very simple way. In ways so that people 'got it'.

I was not a salesperson as such. What seemed to work was that people would tend to recommend me to someone else. Maybe because of the stories I was telling them and they enjoyed them.

He was so successful, it seemed a natural progression to go into business for himself. So he did – many times.

I set up my own financial services business with a number of offices and I now recognize I'm not a good manager. I didn't know that I didn't have the nous to run a business and I lost a lot of money. I lost my shirt.

I went into health clubs. I joined a club and within six weeks I was fitter than I had been for ten years, and then later I ran the New York marathon. So I invested in clubs and lost my shirt again.

People said to me, 'Why don't you stick to what you do best?' I needed to find something that I could become really passionate about and then find a way of making an income out of that.

Cargill realized he had been successful in financial services not because he was a technical expert or a great businessman, but because he was a great storyteller, a great communicator, a great connector. This is what he really loved doing. He hated running businesses. He had no talent for it. That's why they all failed.

I read a book on time management. I was interested in the way the guy wrote it and so I went to see him. That was a major change of direction. I wanted to find out more about what makes people tick.

I became interested in the whole area of motivation. How to help people identify with themselves, things that they should be doing that would give them a chance to look at themselves afresh. I stumbled along, bumping into people, grasping ideas and concepts, and then gradually, as they gathered, I realized that there was something in this.

I saw this thing about 'value of the person' and the words jumped off the page to me. I couldn't go into an organization and say, 'Let me tell you how to run your business' when I hadn't been able to run my own. What I could do I felt, was; if it starts from the individual, then …

Well then, he could use his natural talents, the things he loves doing, to inspire people through stories, to communicate and to connect.

It was a bumpy ride at first, but now I realize it was always about story-telling and it was always about connecting people.

Cargill is now an award-winning motivational speaker and consultant who is doing groundbreaking work on how to identify talent themes in individuals based on the work done by the Gallup Organisation in *Now, Discover Your Strengths*.

He readily admits that if he had properly analyzed his own talents much earlier, his road to a life that he loves would have been less hazardous.

It's only me

'It's only me.' How can people say that? We are all unique and in some way we are all special. We don't always realize in what ways we are special.

When you were conceived there was one egg, but there were something like 250–500 million sperm battling to fertilize that egg and it was you that won. There is a 100 million to 1 chance against you being born, but if you take it back you have grandparents and great-grandparents and the chances of you being here in the form you are is billions to one. You are unique, and no-one can deny that you are a miracle. Most of us don't realise our own uniqueness.

What's changed dramatically in recent times is our ability to identify things that we can't help doing. If people work in areas that are natural to them, they find that they learn more quickly, it's easier and more enjoyable, and the whole thing becomes much more fun for them.

Based on about two million interviews and a raft of research on talent, The Gallup Organization has come up with StrengthsFinder, a web-based questionnaire capable of identifying your key talent themes. Talent is something which is innate, which you do naturally, separate from skill or knowledge, and it is something that every single one of us possesses. In the StrengthsFinder analysis, there are 34 talent themes (see Table 2.1).

Table 2.1 *StrengthFinder's 34 talent themes*

Achiever	Activator	Adaptability
Analytical	Arranger	Belief
Command	Communication	Competition
Connectedness	Context	Deliberative
Developer	Discipline	Empathy
Fairness	Focus	Futuristic
Harmony	Ideation	Inclusiveness
Individualization	Input	Intellection
Learner	Maximizer	Positivity
Relator	Responsibility	Restorative
Self-assurance	Significance	Strategic
Woo		

There is a 32 million to one chance of you having the same five talent themes as somebody else. If you were to take your top eight themes, statistically there is not another person on the planet that has the same talent themes as you.

So we are all rather unique. By finding our talents, and working in ways that allow us to apply them, we can truly do what we love.

For example, my talent themes emerge as:

- **Ideation.** Always looking for connections and intrigued when seemingly disparate phenomena can be linked by an obscure connection.
- **Strategic.** Sees patterns where others see only complexity and, mindful of these patterns, plays out alternative scenarios to find the best route.
- **Futuristic.** A dreamer who sees visions of what could be. Inspires others with visions of the future.
- **Relator.** Enjoys close relationships with other people. Finds deep satisfaction in working hard with others towards a common goal.

- **Connectedness.** Has faith in the connectedness of things. Believes there are few coincidences and that things happen for a reason. Gives others comfort that there is a purpose beyond our humdrum lives.

I found this analysis quite staggering and remarkably accurate and insightful. I have just summarized the descriptions of my talent themes here; StrengthsFinder will give a much more detailed account of each theme. I can see now why my mission to do 'great things with great people' was exactly right for me. It allows me to use my talent themes almost every day – no wonder I love it.

Your first step in doing what you love is to find out what your talent themes are. When you find that you are able to use these every day, you will find true passion in your working life.

Use StrengthsFinder if you wish. Alternatively, think back over your life and identify the times when you felt really alive, excited, passionate or fulfilled. What talents were you using then?

Remember, your talents are natural. They may be quite different from the skills and knowledge that you have acquired over the years. Ask a close friend to be quite open and honest with you. Ask what they think your talents are – use the StrengthsFinder themes to help describe them. When you have found your predominant talent themes, you can begin to think about how you can create a setting in which to apply them.

To do so successfully, you will need a 'sticky ball'. You can't buy one or borrow one. You will have to create your very own.

In the next chapter, I am going to show you how to pull one out of thin air and set it off rolling.

Rolling in the direction of a life that you can love.

3

You are what you believe –
how imagery can transform your life

Jerusalem, 1974. A young Gerald Epstein arrives with his wife at a rented apartment. Along with his luggage, he carries a newspaper that he picked up on the plane. He is unaware that this newspaper will set off a chain of events that will culminate in a small gesture of the hand by a small old lady. A gesture that will change his life irrevocably. A gesture that will lead him to a life that he can love.

I've been interested in imagery all my life. I didn't know that there was a name for it. I had just noticed how often, when I played things over in my mind, they actually came to pass.

Most dramatically, as a child growing up in the inner city, I remember the very first time I saw the countryside. It was a revelation to me, that there were fields with sheep and cows, and that people actually lived there. The effect was so powerful that I can still see that image in my mind today. Over the next 24 years I often revisited this image, thinking that one day I would live in a place like that. Twenty-four years later I did, complete with sheep and cows. It came to pass. It took a long time, but I was young – I got distracted a lot.

Was there a link between the eight-year-old's image and what actually came to pass? Or was it simply coincidence?

According to Epstein these things are no coincidence, and he has had to go to Hell and back in order to stand by his conviction. He need not have done – he had quite a nice life. He says:

I was trained as a conventional physician, and a psychiatrist and psycho-analyst. I was doing very well – I had a practice in New York City, I was publishing in that field and, in 1973, I co-founded *The Journal of Psychiatry and Law*. In 1974, I wangled my way to come over to Jerusalem, because we had published something by the head of psychiatry in there. So I wrote him a letter to ask if I could come as a visiting professor.

They set up an apartment. Beautiful place, beautiful views. Near the hospital, which I didn't do much in, because there was a language barrier and there wasn't much going on forensically that I hadn't done before and that I could connect with.

With little demand on his time, he and his wife had determined that they would meditate. The newspaper from the aeroplane contained an advert for a meditation centre, or Zendo, in Jerusalem. Having always been interested in the philosophies of the East, the Epsteins began to attend.

There was a young man who was sitting with us every day. He asked what we did and I told him I was a psychoanalyst, and he said, 'Oh well, I did that for three years, five days a week in Paris, and it didn't help me at all.'

I met someone here and she works in mental imagery called waking dream therapy, and all my problems disappeared within a month.

Epstein's background and training as a Freudian analyst made him more than just a little cynical. He scoffed at the idea that somebody could resolve those issues so fast if the changes were going to be lasting. He says that 'analysis is a long drawn-out process. It's a macro input for a micro output in truth.' Whereas imagery, he later discovered, 'is a micro input for a macro output'.

Epstein's wife, a journalist, had been working too. 'She was doing an article for a magazine on a social issue in Israel and she was interviewing people from different parts of the world who were living there.' The young man from the Zendo said that he could set up a meeting with a local Algerian woman.

I didn't want to go because I had sat in these interviews and they were quite boring. But a voice came from somewhere and said, 'Go'. It was an imperative 'Go'.

So I followed it. I went outside and said 'Wait, I'm coming with you.' So we got to this place, this house, and it was quite exotic. We passed through a blue gate and then down eight steps to a little garden through a door into an area which was the foyer to this apartment.

After the interview we pulled our chairs closer. She spoke English. I understood at that moment that she was the therapist of the young man.

I said to her, 'I understand that you treated this young man and that he took care of everything in four weeks that he couldn't do in three years. He says he did it through mental imagery and waking dream – I never heard of that.'

And then I had a sudden insight that had never occurred to me before. I had written a paper that was published in an analytical journal on the fundamental rule of psychoanalysis, which is free association: lie on the couch, say whatever comes into your mind, don't edit it, don't censor it.

I said to her, 'You know, Freud wrote a paper in 1912 for young analysts just starting out in their practice, telling them how to begin the treatment, and he said to tell the patient to imagine that you are both on a train – he used the word "imagine" – and that the patient was looking out of the window and describing to you everything that he saw in the countryside as it passed by.

'You know, he gave the rule of free association as an image' – and that occurred to me, it had never entered my mind before, but there it was in black and white.

She looked at me and said, 'In what direction does the train go?' I was thrown off. Paradoxical responses shake your mind.

I had a reflected response. I sat back and became a little tense, I sweated a little bit and my arms were clutching the chair and I'm thinking to myself, what kind of a trick question is this? Trains go in one direction. Then your monkey mind starts. I think, let's see, in Machu Pichu the trains go up and I've been to Switzerland where the trains go up, and then I thought, well, I have to give her an answer and I don't want to give the 'wrong answer', because you have to say the 'right thing'. So I sat back and said in the way that doctors hedge their bets with patients – you give the medical answer which is 'not infrequently' or 'most often', so that they don't panic – 'Most frequently trains go like –', and I made a movement with my hand straight ahead.

She looked at me and moved her arm in a vertical movement and asked, 'And if we change the direction?'

To this day Epstein finds it hard to put into words what went through his mind at that moment. He had one of those 'aha' experiences – what he refers to as an epiphany. He feels that somehow the vertical movement lifted him from the horizontal hold of the given, the everyday patterns of cause and effect. He realized what therapy was all about – to go beyond the given.

Following that, coming back to reality, I had the thought that I'm no longer an analyst, I'm no longer a psychiatrist, I'm no longer an MD in the conventional way. That's done. I've found something here that I think is in truth.

She saw the thoughts that went on and she said, 'You found this interesting, didn't you?' I said of course and she said, 'Would you like to learn more?' And I said of course. She said to come back the next morning at eight o'clock.

And so I began my apprenticeship with her. I gave up everything that I had learned and studied in a moment, that epiphanic moment, and trained in this way, which I guess you could call spiritual healthcare. That was how it all started.

He applied the imagery techniques to healthcare, his professional calling – but he is adamant that it can be applied to any situation or walk of life.

If I was an accountant, I would have unfolded it in my accountancy work. If I was a shoe-maker, I would have unfolded it in my shoe-making work.

Whatever your calling is, you can apply these techniques. So I wasn't a clinician and someone dedicated to this tradition, I was unfolding this tradition through my clinical work. You unfold through the calling that you follow in your life. So you're not an astrologer and interested in western spirituality: your astrological understanding would flow out of your dedication to this practice.

I apprenticed for 9 years with her. I went back 13 or 14 times, and in the course of doing that I 'got my wings', so to speak – I graduated. I've been doing this work for the past 30 years, since 1974, and my relationship with her continued as a friend for this period until she died in 1993 at the age of 94¾. Her name was Colette Aboulker-Muscat.

She taught me this 'way of the imaginal' and its application to everyday life: topical, difficult issues that people encounter, and also how it is used as a practice of spirit. It can be used to be an interaction, so it has a unique foundation because you can use it either way.

Delighted with his new calling, Epstein returned to New York to practice. However, he met with a hostile reception.

I got an awful reaction from my colleagues. I became ostracized. Remember, I was part of the analytic community, and I had a whole bevy of analytic colleagues who were referring to me. I would attend meetings, I was writing papers and so on.

Once it came to light that I was doing this work, the phone stopped ringing, I stopped getting referrals and I was told I was crazy, and it was interesting, because my analyst and I became very close friends. He got calls from people at the Institute threatening him with being ostracized himself if he continued his friendship with me. So they came down very heavy and hard.

I lost everything. I became destitute financially. I had to take a job in a clinic monitoring people who had been put on medication.

I lost my income, I lost my friends, my family thought I had gone crazy, my wife was under a great deal of tension about the shift that I had made so abruptly without discussing it with her – I felt like I was choked. I would have lost my home had I not got this job. It was this job that allowed me to continue living and paying rent. We scrimped along. We just managed.

He was all at sea professionally and would never regain his position within the analytic community. Then things began to shift.

Other people started taking notice of me. When you do this, and make a space, new people come into your life. As you discard your old paradigms and belief systems, new people start to enter into your existence.

I began to develop a new community. In '74 I had two patients in analysis and I gave them this method. They told me their 'night dream' and I told them to go back and explore it in this imaginal way, to go back and describe their experience – what they found, what they felt, what they heard. Of course the waking dream is a way in which you explore consciousness. You use the night dream as a jumping-off point to enter into a deeper state of consciousness. The waking dream helps you find out who you are and what you can do to change your life.

Now these two people did that. They were open to it. They had trust. Within a month they both finished their analysis, just like that guy in Jerusalem.

He was the only person practising waking dream therapy in New York. In those days, there was no fax and no Internet, and letters to Jerusalem took 17 days. He was alone.

In his most difficult moments, he asked his teacher Madame Alboulker-Muscat how he would survive – or as he puts it, 'I said how, what, where, blah, blah, blah'.

Her reply was simple: 'You teach, and everything will come to you through teaching.' One of his patients subsequently met the person she had been longing for. He happened to run a meditation centre. When she told him of Epstein's imagery work, he asked him to come and teach it.

As a consequence, I opened my own school. People got to know about my work. It was authorized by the State of New York and it still exists. They give certification in this work. Students started to come, and as they did, other people got to know about my work, people came to get help for physical and emotional problems.

I wrote two books in 1980 and 1981, then several other books followed, and 25 papers, and I've become known.

In the ensuing years, thousands of people have been helped through the use of mental imagery. It seems that it can be used for anything from getting a job or finding a mate to dealing with a raft of physical and mental conditions.

I got a call from a woman who was going to have a Caesarean. She had a breach. The doctors told her it's impossible to deliver the baby from below and that they'll have to do a Caesarean. So I give her an image to rotate the baby, so that it comes out in the proper position. When they examine her to do the section, they find the baby is in the proper position, so the baby's delivered from below.

The interesting thing is that in 30 years with all the physical illness that we have helped with, not once has a doctor contacted me to find out what happened. In my students' work it is the same. One brilliant student works in cancer, where the doctors have given some degree of credence to this work of changing a medical condition.

They tell the patient, 'If you believe it – good.' That's great; they are using my very principle: if you believe it – good. What you believe you will create.

Some of the sceptics feel that imagery does not produce lasting change. Epstein is bullish on this.

> A guy came to me with atrophy of his optic nerve and he wasn't given a driver's licence by New York State. We did work and he regained his vision. He worked on this 13 years ago. He still has his vision. It's lasting. How long is lasting?
>
> We published two papers: one about the patients' experience, one about what happened to their pulmonary function. They were followed for four months and some for a year. Using imagery, nearly 50% of patients got off medication without any deterioration in pulmonary function.

It seems that what you see is what you believe, and what you believe is what you are, and even your body can take on board this message.

I was interested in why Epstein took such a massive risk, why he flew in the face of his profession, why he carried on when the successful life he had built was crumbling around him. Without a pause he is clear about it.

> Faith. Why would I give everything up and trade it in at that moment after an inspirational thought? I had faith in her. I went through an experience which was indescribable by words. I had faith in her and what she was going to teach me.

He is adamant that all of us can step out into the unknown, if we have absolute faith in what we are doing.

> You realize that the invisible reality gives us what we need. It provides for us, as Shakespeare said, 'measure for measure'. What we give out is what we get back, says the Gospel, and the universe is around to be there for you all the time. What she taught me was how to make contact with it.

Imagery has transformed the lives of Gerald Epstein and thousands of others who have worked with him, but how does it work, and how can we use it in seeking a life that we can love?

> The imagery process is the natural language of the mind. It's very simple, in truth – once you learn about the principles of spirit, it becomes much easier.

People can take themselves out of their own misery if they choose to. We are not educated as to how to do that; the educational system does not allow you to be free. The institutions that run us don't want us to be free, they want to dominate and control our lives and support their needs, the shift to become free. Very simply, change your belief systems. Imagery is effectively a belief system given form. In a state of consciousness you create a belief.

Let me give an example. Somebody comes along and says, 'I'll never get out of this misery that I'm in.' I tell them they are getting out of this misery that they are in – now how does it look as an image?

They say, 'I see myself climbing up out of a pit. I have a rope ladder and as I come up, I see light, and I come up into the light.'

They have an experience similar to mine. They see that they have the means inwardly to change the belief and it has an image associated with it. They do an inward process of action that gets manifested as your outer experience.

What you believe you will manifest as your outer experience.

In other words, if you use an image to create a new belief for yourself – for example, that you are going to be successful in earning your living by doing what you love – your mind and body will begin to take action to make the belief into reality.

Epstein now disputes the traditional Freudian approach of 'what I experience creates what I believe'.

This is what I was labouring with under Freud – the experiences of my childhood determine what I become like as an adult. In other words, my experience becomes my reality.

We are saying that what I *believe* becomes my experience and my reality.

What do you have available to you that cannot be taken from you by any dictator or tyrant? Your ability to believe.

How to use your beliefs to manifest change

The great thing about using imagery to create beliefs is that anyone can do it. It doesn't require any expensive technical equipment or knowledge and it is, in the overall scheme of things, not particularly time-consuming.

In his 30 years doing imagery work, Dr Epstein has not yet come across a single person who has been unable to create a mental image. We can all do it. The question is, how do we do it successfully?

In Epstein's analysis, it is all very simple. Look at your life as a garden that needs to be tended. You are a life-gardener entrusted with creating your own 'reality garden'. To create a new reality for yourself, you have to attend to three functions: weeding, seeding and harvesting.

Of course, gardens that are full of weeds cannot yield a proper harvest, so you have to work to get rid of these before you begin to plant new seeds. Negative beliefs and emotions must be cleared away, if any new seed is to grow properly. Mental imagery can be used to create positive beliefs and emotions, so that new seeds can be planted in fertile ground.

Now we can establish and nurture our new seeds by visualizing our new reality. If you want success, how does it look; if you want contribution, how do you see it? What does a life that you can love look like?

Epstein's advice is to spend a short time revisiting this image every morning for 21 days, then taking 7 days off, then beginning the cycle again. This cycle parallels a biological rhythm that is present in all of us, particularly women, who experience the cycle of three weeks of hormonal regulation, followed by a week of menstruation.

We make our beliefs our reality and our reality becomes our experience. In Epstein's words:

> That's all. You've planted a seed, nurtured it watered it. Now the seed has to take fruit and grow. That's how it works. It's simple.

There are four things to do to prepare the mind for mental imaging work: intention, quieting, cleansing and changing.

Intention

Always begin by defining and clarifying the intention – what you want to achieve from the exercise. For example, 'My book is going to be a massive success and a valuable tool for thousands of people.'

Quieting

There are two types of quieting: external and internal. You don't need to go into a monastery to do imaging, but do get away from jarring sounds. Some sounds, such as birdsong or the gentle lapping of the sea, can actually be helpful.

Internal quieting is about achieving a relaxed state. Not too relaxed – you don't want to go into deep relaxation – you want to achieve a state of 'heightened wakefulness'. Take a deep breath and breathe out two or three times consecutively.

Cleansing

To get the best from imaging we must be willing to make an effort to cleanse ourselves inwardly. According to Epstein, 'every moral or ethical indiscretion is registered in our bodies and can adversely influence the workings of our physical and mental lives'.

We have to make a conscious effort to 'clean up our act' in order to properly open the imaginal eye. We need to look inwardly at ourselves, be honest, get rid of our delusions and consider how we relate to others.

Changing

Changing is about opening yourself up to the inevitability of change. We have a tendency to try to hold on to what we consider to be 'good situations'. By holding on ever tighter, we ourselves tighten up, resist the possibility that change might bring pain, and run head on into the very pain we are trying to avoid.

Many people who have stayed in jobs too long, been made redundant or found themselves in a loveless marriage, will identify with this. Holding on to something that is impermanent but pretending it is permanent can only lead to trouble and, according to Epstein, 'most often the form the trouble takes is a physical ailment'.

Openness to change is one of the keys to the way of the imaginal.

I have a dream

Today we have become so focused on logical left-brain thinking – words, numbers and rational thought – that many people have lost faith in their ability to achieve things through intuition and picture-making. This is right-brain activity, which we need to exercise much more so that it reverts to its natural place of equality with logical thinking.

Many people working in large and small organizations become fixated with logical approaches. These become embedded in strategies and plans, and in turn become a crutch to the extent that without such documents, people feel anxious and exposed.

Great leadership and achievement can be brought about by the way of the imaginal. When Martin Luther King took to the steps of the Lincoln Memorial in Washington DC on August 28, 1963, he didn't say 'I have a strategic plan', did he?

He had a dream – a waking dream. A dream that he described as an image:

> When we let freedom ring, when we let it ring from every village and every hamlet, from every state and every city, we will be able to speed up that day when all of God's children, black men and white men, Jews and Gentiles, Protestants and Catholics, will be able to join hands and sing in the words of the old Negro spiritual: 'Free at last! Free at last! Thank God Almighty, we are free at last!'

On that day in 1963, 250,000 protesters saw an image of freedom. It was an image that was to shake the nation and created a belief in a new future, a belief that was acted out in experience, a belief which became a reality as equal rights and social justice crept into the American psyche.

He began his speech with another piece of imagery:

> In a sense we have come to our nation's capital to cash a cheque. When the architects of our republic wrote the magnificent words of the Constitution and the Declaration of Independence, they were signing a promissory note to which every American was to fall heir …
>
> So we've come to cash this cheque – a cheque that will give us upon demand the riches of freedom and the security of justice.

In the history of mankind, that was an almighty cheque that he cashed that day. And it all began with a waking dream – an image.

The way of the imaginal

Gerald Epstein's story can give hope to all of us who want to earn a living by doing what we love. He went against his logical mind and the dogma of his professional training; inexplicably, he backed his intuition.

He had to keep his faith when his fellow practitioners conspired to almost bring him to professional and financial ruin. He had to maintain his belief when everyone around him, including his friends and family, believed that he was going crazy.

He was helped by his own waking dreams, by his imaginings, and new doors began to open. He created a new space for himself and new people were attracted towards it.

I'm glad that he did. He is living proof that if you are truly passionate about something and you maintain your faith and belief, you can earn your living by doing what you love – even when you are selling the 'waking dream', an extraordinary concept that hardly anyone has ever heard of before.

I'm also glad that he did, because his 30 years of experience of mental imagery helps us to understand how we can use imagery in our daily lives, and how we can prepare ourselves for doing what we love.

His life is so different now.

When I first met my teacher in Jerusalem I was falling asleep. I couldn't stay awake – I was burned out.

Years of constantly hearing the [patients'] droning of the same false beliefs and the stories that were being told to account for their lives, and the things that were supposed to be responsible, and the blaming and complaining. My life is 180 degrees different. My life is dedicated to this work.

I'm optimistic, cheerful, humorous – I've got nothing to complain about.

He is indeed a man who loves what he does.

4

The sticky ball principle
and the power of connection

On September 11, 1973, General Augusto Pinochet led a military coup against the ruling Allende government. Allende died in the fighting in the presidential palace in Santiago.

Over the next few years more than 3,000 supporters of the Allende regime were killed. Pinochet was also responsible for thousands of people being tortured and large numbers were forced into exile.

One man who was tortured and exiled was Santiago Bell, an educationalist, philosopher and artist. He would eventually make his way to London, but not before spending several years imprisoned in horrendous conditions.

At around the same time, a young Yorkshireman, Andrew Mawson, was beginning a journey: a journey away from a stable, respectable career path, and towards a life that he could love.

He would eventually make his way to London, but not before he had grappled with some of what he calls the 'why?' questions.

In time a connection would be made, which in turn would establish more connections, and would illustrate how the 'sticky ball' principle can help make something from nothing.

I first met Andrew Mawson when a colleague told me she had invited a reverend to speak at a conference we were holding. I thought she had taken leave of her senses – a reverend?

Instantly I was struck by Andrew's passion, by what he had done and how he had done it, and by the remarkable life that he is able to live – and earn a living from. He is, to be frank, a highly irreverent reverend.

Over the years we have often worked together. He has pushed me to think bigger, better, harder, sideways and upways, so that at times I seemed to be meeting myself coming back.

In doing so we've achieved things that we are proud of. I have had the opportunity to observe him at close quarters and untangle some of the principles that are vital in earning your living by doing what you love.

Andrew has probably exhibited all of the principles of the formula that I promised to unfold in his work. However, I want to focus on something that I think he is exceptional at: the 'sticky ball' principle and the power of connection.

He left school at the age of 16, simply because he found it boring.

I got interested in how things worked rather than why. I got a chance to become a telecommunications engineer with the GPO, and at that time my parents were very pleased, because at that time parents believed that this was a job for life. Three hundred people applied for these jobs and I managed to get one.

He didn't realize it at the time, but the training turned out to be really useful for someone who was later to be termed as a 'social entrepreneur'.

You did technology, dug the roads, got egg sandwiches for blokes who climbed the posts, you went into people's houses installing telephones and three years of doing all those different jobs taught one a lot about a lot. Entrepreneurs, I always think, are people who need to know a lot about a lot of different things.

And so it was quite a good training, although it was obviously meant to be training me to become a telecommunications engineer for the next 40 years.

He did qualify and could conceivably be installing telephones today, but a meeting with a clergyman at his local church began to open up other possibilities.

I met a clergyman who began to give a very different picture of what the church was about, and asked rather interesting questions about why, rather than how, things worked, and I thought I'd like to know much more about that.

One was coming across parts of Christianity that didn't make sense of the work situation and the world as I was discovering it, and I thought, I actually need to understand this for myself. Naïvely I thought that the only way to do that is to go and train to be a clergyman.

So I ended up going to Northern Baptist College to meet the principal, Michael Taylor, who was a very clever guy – I thought I had never met someone so clever before. He began to ask really difficult questions.

He wanted to go and suck in more of this, but the College would not recognize Andrew's qualifications. He needed to get three A Levels in 30 weeks. So, quite simply, he did.

Suddenly education was quite exciting. At school I'd got bored with it, but now that it was something I had chosen to do, it became quite exciting.

Being at college with a person that's asking all sorts of exciting questions and not letting anything go unexamined was a very good time to be there. They always say that in your life you are lucky to have one or two good teachers who really influence you – well, I've had two. Michael Taylor was the first one.

Eric Blakebrough, an off-the-wall reverend in Kingston upon Thames, was to become his second great teacher. Eric had developed a drugs project and an all-night hostel, and had rung up the college principal saying that he was looking for someone to join him who was unusual. He was immediately given Mawson's number.

We got on a train and Eric picked us up in a yellow Morgan, and I thought, 'This is the boy. This is the man.' We hit it off immediately – it was exactly the right thing. In a sense, Michael Taylor at the Northern Baptist College sorted my head out and Eric began to show me that you could do a lot with a little, and what it meant to be an entrepreneurial clergyman. He was challenging the health service and the clergy. They all thought he was awkward and difficult, and I didn't – I thought he was spot on, actually.

Then something happened that established one of Mawson's defining characteristics: if something matters, get in there and do something about it – what works is what counts.

Archbishop Romero was murdered in Central America on March 24, 1980 by a gunman who broke into a cancer hospital and shot him dead. Many of us were very aware that no-one had heard at that point what was going on there. I felt so outraged at this that I said, 'We are not just going to let this rest – we are going to make something of this.'

We ran an all-night club at Kaleidoscope for people with drug dependency and I decided we would create a national campaign there and then. The world became aware of it. I went on the first British Council of Churches delegation to Central America, where we met key ministers in El Salvador and Nicaragua, and the Secretary of State for Human Rights in Washington. I began to believe that big things could happen out of small places – that the micro could really be the key to the macro.

It all had to do with what you believed was possible and if you didn't believe it, no-one else would believe it.

All of a sudden, people began to stick to it and began to have a momentum.

It began to teach me some things about putting a major national campaign together and gaining momentum, creating a kind of 'sticky ball' that other people began to stick to. There are moments. My instinct was telling me that the moment was right. It wasn't thought out of some business plan or some clever analytical document, it was just me following my instinct. Over the years my instinct, about 90% of the time, has turned out to be a fairly reliable guide.

Mawson was getting noticed, and after four years working in Kingston, he had a nice life and people wanted him to stay.

We really liked it, but I thought maybe what I should be doing is taking my cumulative experience and putting it on the map somewhere. One of the clergy who had been to Central America with me came to see me and said, 'There's this pastor who dropped dead last week in his church in Bromley by Bow. Why don't you come and look at it?'

I went over to look at this derelict church, and I met one or two of the church members, who were quite eccentric, and I liked it. My instinct told me this place has nothing but these raw assets, I could sense I'd got all sorts of complications, and I thought maybe this is where I should be. It would be too comfortable to stay where I was. So with a risk, really, we managed to put a deal together for two years' funding and we made the move. There wasn't a church house so we lived in a housing association flat.

Bromley by Bow in East London was right at the top of the league for deprivation, ill health and poverty. Mawson soon became frustrated that the voluntary and public sectors seemed to do a lot of talking, and not that much in terms of making a difference to people's everyday lives.

I began to realize if you really want to bring change into things, this idea of passing through on the three-year *Guardian* advert is a complete waste of time really. What you have to do is dig in or move out. Move in, stay there and get to know the detail. People respect you and you can play a major role.

When it was time to go to Bromley, I realized that the only way to really have an impact was to stay there a generation, not move through. I've watched too many people moving through. People who did not have an entrepreneurial mindset, they had a careerist mindset and ideological ideas about poverty that they had picked up from university from people who had never met anyone in those circumstances. They had certainly never built anything, so one began to see the contradictions.

Nowadays I can analyze it a lot more. At that point, I sensed that my training had been preparing me for something like this. I could sense that it was a place of opportunity that required a different sort of mindset from what I was seeing there. I wandered around the area and came across the voluntary sector having endless management meetings, loads of ideology and they all hated each other. They endlessly talked equal opportunities. Everything about that was unhealthy, in my view. Then you would come across Karen, a single parent who had three kids and lived in a tower block, who said, 'I don't want to join a management committee, but what we really need around here is a decent nursery and a decent health facility.'

When I arrived, I realized that I had a derelict church, 12 old people, £400 in the bank and a leaking roof. I remember being taken by Lillian into one of the areas where it was leaking. There was no light and the windows were boarded up. I could feel the water beneath my feet and sort of paddled to the end of this room, where there was a piano. I lifted the lid and the keys were totally solid and a little voice from Lillian said, 'And yes, Andrew, I polish it every Thursday.' What you saw there was the link between the dereliction of the space and a person's life that was also in complication, each working themselves out on each other in this amorphous mass that was Tower Hamlets.

What I began to realise was that all this theoretical talk and ideology in the voluntary sector wasn't in touch with customers like Karen at all. What they were hearing from these parents was massive frustration because nothing was happening and nobody knew what to do about it. Maybe in the middle of that there was an opportunity.

So he set out building relationships with people on the ground – 'in the micro', as he likes to say. A chance occurrence brought about a connection which was to prove to be a catalyst.

I was still engaged in Central America. I had to go and speak in Birmingham. I was in a car with a journalist who told me that there was this bloke in her house called Santiago Bell who was putting up shelves but he is a fantastic joiner. He'd worked with Paulo Ferrer, the famous educationalist in Chile, and got thrown out during the coup. He was looking for a workshop.

I just said, 'Get him to come and see me.' I'm in my little vestry in an empty church and this guy walks in with a face that looks like a sculpture, but a sculpture that's been to Hell and back. I began to listen and thought, 'Oh, my God – what has gone on here?' He just wanted somewhere to build a workshop, so I said, 'Here's a room at the front of the church – no-one's using it, have that.'

He began to go round skips and find timber and began to build these fantastic workbenches with nothing. I thought, blimey, this guy really is it. Then he began moving in some of the sculptures he was working on, these fantastic wooden sculptures, and of course other people began to come into the building and see this stuff and he connected with them.

As Santiago Bell created connections, he began to unveil his philosophy and drew on some of the things he had learned whilst imprisoned in Chile. For Mawson, it was an education in creativity and human spirit.

He began to teach me that artists have a way of thinking about the world that can be really important for community development. In Chile, he and his wife had taken street children into their house and at one point had 30 living with them. He was an old person now who had this deep sense of how you build communities. And whilst he was too old to do it, he began to teach me a way of thinking creatively about the world.

A little team began to grow. He connected well with artists who were living locally in squats and they got on well with Ethel, who was in the congregation. I had begun to try to connect with bits of the voluntary sector and found them so hopeless, so distorted, that eventually a few of us said, 'Why don't we just do it ourselves? Let's take these assets and build on them.'

All sorts of people began to join us. Santiago rebuilt his workshop and rebuilt his life. The way he survived in prison was by creating some order with bread and water. Here we were in East London in a pretty chaotic situation. Santiago used to say things like 'keep the pace' and 'create the order'. As we began to think about the church we built these candle holders and we moved all the church and created the round.

Now worship was performed in a small central area of the church called 'the round'. Empty rooms in this derelict old church suddenly were coming to life, and more and more connections between people and ideas were springing up.

The idea was of creating a sense of rhythm connecting creativity to community. Santiago's view was that there is no such thing as a straight line – everything always bends. Little bits of flair like this began to create the stickiness. My view was that the micro is the clue about the macro. And other people began to stick …

Santiago arrived. Janet arrived with this idea of developing a dance school and we said yes. Santiago and a few of us said, 'Why not just say yes to everybody? What have you got to lose?' Fortunately, the church members joined in that. So Janet moved in, we charged a bit of rent, formed a relationship and she grew it.

The voluntary sector jumped up and down and said, 'This is terrible, she's going to charge these kids', and I'm saying, 'Well, there are no grants – let's just see what happens.' People bought into it. They realized that Janet had been a professional dancer, knew about how the industry worked and created discipline for the kids – they had uniforms.

Eventually, one child was offered a place at The Royal Ballet, and you suddenly realized that life was coming to bear with discipline and order and all those things that Santiago talked about.

Creativity and order. In year six it grew too big and moved into its own building with about 35 staff.

Eve Good appeared with some other parents who had been running a nursery in a house down the street that they had grown too big for. By now, Santiago had developed all the derelict space in the church and the only bit left was the main church space. We went in and they said that it would be fantastic for their nursery; I laughed and said that it was a bit more complex than that: 'There is me and these 12 old people that do this eccentric thing every Sunday called worship, and this is the only bit of our church we have left.' One of the women said, 'You can't even afford to decorate and heat it – why don't you move out and we move in?' Some people might have been quite threatened by this blunt suggestion. Actually, I thought it was a really creative thought.

So my instinct was not to be offended, it was, 'let's become mates'. Let's form a partnership that brings together you lot, Ethel, me and Sue, who lives in a squat. Let's get Gordon the architect to come up with a plan to rip out the whole of this church and build the canopy, the church, the art gallery, the first integrated nursery in Britain – so you don't just put 25 kids from the 'at risk' register together, you have some places for doctors and teachers who pay the going rate because then they make demands about the quality and force the quality upwards – and some places for Bengali children that would allow us to economically run 11 crèches a week. If you put all the monies together, it makes a sustainable business.

The church was transformed into a multi-use space, filled with beautiful art and built with the best materials. It became a hive of activity for all kinds of people, from all kinds of faiths and backgrounds, whether or not they had any interest in religion.

We began to do it and a group of relationships began to happen. Then Shirley arrives – the expert from Social Services who has never heard such nonsense in her life: 'You can't possibly have a church and a nursery because there's all these rules and regulations.' She put her hand in her bag and pulled out the encyclopaedia of a thousand reasons why it couldn't be done. I remember these meetings – she used to come with another person. She used to say things and he used to nod. And you thought, the public sector is paying for both of these people – why can't one of them come?

We were getting very excited by our plans and they were looking completely unpersuaded, saying it's all impossible. East End parents can get really cross, and I'm saying, 'Look, you've got a real problem because these people want it to happen and you are not seeing it, so I've got to see your boss.'

When rules don't work you break them. Of course, this is complete heresy to them.

The Director came down and fortunately for me he had a more entrepreneurial headset. By chance he was there at the right time. He said, 'Look, I can build ten of these for the cost of one I have just built on the Isle of Dogs. Can we change the design of the babies' sleeping area and the toilets? By being flexible we built it and now run three other nurseries. Just recently, the [former] Secretary of State for Health John Reid and Government Minister Tessa Jowell opened the new one, which is a 48-place nursery with a performance area and 10 flats built out of the same hand-made bricks used at Glyndbourne opera house.

The lesson is, if we had listened to the officials, we wouldn't now have a nursery business.

Things were now moving and a lady called Sue Fox developed the Pie In The Sky Café: not the trestle, table and teabag affair that you would associate with a church hall, but a standalone glass and chrome building that would not be out of place in the West End, let alone the East End.

We began to think that it was ridiculous that all the money in the area goes through the system back to Essex and Kent. All these professionals come in on a Monday, and they've all been to university and are wonderful on social justice and equity, and they come in and they do things to people. They earn £30,000-a-year salaries and they get on trains every night and they leave. They leave taking all the money with them, leaving behind a massive dependency culture that seemed to me rather contradictory.

So we began to think, why don't we do our own community care and care for each other?

We got to know Billy, who had become unemployed because he got epilepsy once every six years, and because of health and safety rules he couldn't work on a building site. The cost to the state is immense: he's in and out of the doctor's all the time, his life's falling apart, his marriage is falling apart. We have a derelict three-acre park behind us and he's into parks, so our message is, 'Here is a pick axe, Billy, just go and dig up the Tarmac – let's just do it'. Bit by bit a community care thing began to happen without any money. Everything with us began without any money, just an idea, because money follows ideas.

About four or five years in we got a bit of money – various trusts liked it and said 'We are going to help you.' Then Jean Viles was introduced to us, a 35-year-old mother dying of cancer with two kids aged 16 and 2 sleeping in the same bed in what was clearly a very complicated situation.

We soon realized that the State's response to this was to have four social workers all writing reports about her, which was pretty useless because she couldn't read them anyway. Jackie, a local mum, got to know Jean, and realized she needed to be bathed, and went in every morning and bathed her, got her into community care, and we cared for her for the last six months of her life.

We realized there was something quite serious going on here. We decided to keep a very detailed record of what has gone on. When it came to the enquiry into her death, the professionals were all a bit snobby: 'Well, we weren't sure about whether this happened or that happened.' Jackie pulled out a diary and they could not believe that this working class mother had every detail and time in the diary.

As they tried to pull the wool, the diary contradicted them. I had to do the funeral and it was very emotional. The press arrived and it all appeared in the papers. The Health Authority were jumping up and down.

I'm called in to a senior-level meeting at the Royal London Hospital and they are all going around the table, just like the Climbié enquiry into the black child that died in the bath, all justifying why they had done or not done certain things to Jean.

So I listened for about three-quarters of an hour and stopped the meeting. Sometimes in your life you have to bang the table. I said, 'I've had enough of this conversation. It is all about you guys protecting your backs. It's not about Jean Viles, who was the customer. If you ran a business like this you would be bankrupt in three weeks.'

At which point, fortunately, the cancer consultant exploded and said to the GP, 'I released this woman into your care – why did you not tell me about this?' Answer: 'Because your fax number had changed.'

Then of course it all begins to crack open and you get two hours of who's not spoken to whom. I just sit and watch, and it was like spaghetti all over the table. The truth was coming out.

Mawson and his team went away angry and determined to turn something bad into something good. Then, some weeks later, the Health Authority asked them to come back to meet with them.

We get called back, by which point we had a plan. We proposed that we would build a health centre owned by the patients, develop the park and build housing for people with care needs.

I thought they would go with it. The senior health people looked at me as if I had said we were going to build a nuclear weapons site in the park.

The mindset was 'we run health'. Instead of them coming back with nine other ideas, it was all about 'we must stop this', not 'we must build something'. It was, 'We must stop this because we are in power, we are in charge.'

Mawson continued to battle with the Health Authority for a further three years, continually meeting blockages – and this in one of the unhealthiest neighbourhoods in the whole of Britain. Then one day he got a call from the then Secretary of State for Health Dr Brian Mawhinney, who had heard about the stand-off and wanted to come and have a look.

He turns up. The ministerial car arrives and I open the back door – and there's no one in the back seat. I'm thinking, did he forget to get in?

I notice him walking through the streets, and I think, this guy is not so stupid – he's sniffing out what is going on. I made sure he felt my frustration. Two and a half weeks later, a letter arrived instructing the Chief Executive of the Health Authority to give three years' funding, two members of staff and to have it in place within 30 days.

Ten years later I asked Brian Mawhinney what happened to him after his visit. He said, 'I had a hundred civil servants telling me why I shouldn't get involved.' I said to him, 'What did you say?' He said, 'This is why I came into politics and this is the decision I am taking.'

Mawson says that Mawhinney's actions, which were extraordinary in terms of a Minister getting involved in the micro, offer an important lesson for all.

Brian Mawhinney was very critical. He took responsibility for a decision, which caused Hell when he did it but it broke the egg.

Take personal responsibility. So many systems are about not taking responsibility.

Today, the Bromley by Bow Healthy Living Centre has an income in excess of £2 million pounds a year, employs 100 local people and its centrepiece is the new integrated health facility set in Billy's three-acre park. Over 125 different activities take place every week and it now enjoys world renown as a model of how to rebuild communities and provide truly integrated services.

Some chance meetings, an open and creative philosophy, a message that became like a sticky ball, and the nurturing of connections and relationships: that is how it was done. Nobody could have foreseen what would have happened. It emerged and grew.

> You begin to grow a group of people who buzz off each other. They emerge – like gardens, they grow and develop. If you encourage it, some roses come up.
>
> I'm not persuaded by this idea that we know what it will be like in ten years' time, or that it's all in our business plan. It's like our children: how do we know what our children will be like in ten years?
>
> Visions emerge. Take entrepreneurs and artists: if an artist is confronted by a bit of clay that looks a bit odd, he will take hold of it and produce something beautiful. Entrepreneurs do that with problems.

Of course, it has not all been plain sailing, and one of the important things is to create a culture of experimentation, where risk and failure are accepted.

> I think we have failures and problems every day. All of us. The critical question is, can we take hold of it now and deal with it. I remember in the early days the voluntary sector would say, 'Oh we can't decide that until the next management committee meeting, which is six weeks away.'
>
> So that small problem is massive in six weeks' time. We need to empower people to decide now. Take responsibility and turn the problem into an opportunity.

Characteristically, Mawson is taking on new responsibility. He is now President of Community Action Network (CAN), an organization dedicated to finding, supporting and connecting people who want to use business skills to tackle some of our most pressing social problems. All over the country, these 'social entrepreneurs' are applying creativity, connection and the sticky ball principle to create jobs, tackle debt, improve healthcare, create new educational settings, develop enterprise and so much more.

> In business, I think I would have got a bit bored of just making money. There's nothing wrong with making money, I don't have a problem with

that – but I would have got bored. I always had a sense that I needed to do something else.

What really excites me is building communities. Human beings, if they can connect in a certain way and form relationships, can become amazingly powerful things.

If you start from people and their passion, if government would allow this to happen and dump ideas of equity and fairness in their purest form, we would get healthier people, people who learn because they want to. And once you get people's passions going, you get 120% commitment. You would get new businesses flowering, communities and relationships that are very strong. But in a very different way.

You would rebuild a society built around passion. Whereas what we are doing at the moment is building a theory of a society

---

He is an irreverent reverend who believes in passion, he loves what he does and believes we all could and all should.

The sticky ball principle

Whatever you choose to do to earn your living, you will inevitably need to attract people to you: customers, collaborators, partners, funders, employees, suppliers and so on.

Andrew Mawson created what he calls a 'sticky ball', which, as it rolled, attracted more people that wanted to stick to it. As it became bigger, yet more people began to stick to it, even people who initially were resistant.

He trained as a preacher. If you were to watch him in action he infects people with a kind of virus by weaving together great stories. He tells them very well, with genuine belief and passion. He also tells them often.

His stories have such appeal because they are not great expositions of macro theories; they are rooted in reality, in the micro, and they allow people to identify with the issues.

They involve real people and real situations, they use metaphor and they invariably paint a picture of a better future if we engage with his latest wacky idea.

In short, these stories create mental images: images that play over and over again in the minds of the people who are touched by them. In doing so, they are, as Gerald Epstein points out, creating new beliefs, new experiences and new realities.

That is exactly what happened in Bromley by Bow for Santiago, who rebuilt his life, Sue Fox, who developed the Pie In The Sky café, Eve Good and the mothers that developed the nursery, Janet and her dance school, Billy and his park, and dozens of others.

These people stuck to the sticky ball, and as they created their new beliefs, experiences and realities, the story got bigger, richer, stickier and the ball began to roll.

Consider Andrew Mawson's comment: 'Everything with us began without any money, just an idea, because money follows ideas.' Sticky balls create something out of nothing. When you consider how you are to earn your living by doing what you love, you must not consider a lack of money as an obstacle.

Andrew Mawson and the Bromley by Bow community transformed a derelict church with £400 in the bank to a state-of-the-art integrated healthy living centre turning over £2 million a year. They were not led by a business plan; the sticky ball was the engine of change.

We're going on a bear hunt

When I had set out to earn a living by doing what I loved – 'great things with great people' – I wondered how I could explain to people what I do.

I imagined going to some marketing agency and seeing them come up with a brochure, just like everybody else's brochure. It would probably begin with a mission statement: 'We aim to be the provider of choice for integrated personal and organizational development, delivering greater leverage and adding value for our clients.'

What? Who would want to stick to that? I began to think about how I would describe what I would do. Over the preceding years I had spent many nights reading a story to my children called *We're Going on a Bear Hunt*. It's the story of how a family sets off in search of a bear, only to come up against a series of obstacles. Often I had thought that this was a good metaphor for life, and that my job in doing great things with great people was to help them break through their obstacles. I was amazed when I opened Charles Leadbeater's book *Living on Thin Air* to find that he had used this theme for one of his chapters. So I set up a company called Bearhunt, and used a simple story to describe what it is about. Here is the story, which I still use today.

Why Bearhunt?

If you're familiar with the children's book *We're Going on a Bear Hunt*, you'll know. In it, a family sets out to meet a bear, only to face a series of daunting obstacles: deep mud, a cold river, a dark forest, a violent storm. At each one, the family are united in their resolve: 'We can't go under it. We can't go over it. We'll have to go through it.'

That is the challenge most of us face today. Whether working in the public, private or voluntary sectors, we will be more dependent upon skills and knowledge in order to steel ourselves to press on. We will have to live with increasing uncertainty of what lies ahead, knowing that retreat offers no alternative.

Bearhunt is about helping to create the spirit, knowledge, skills, creativity and desire to enable you to overcome your obstacles.

The future is both exciting and frightening. We have to go forward, we have to be positive, so … we're going on a bear hunt.

This simple little story was the beginning of my sticky ball. It was something that I believed in and I enjoyed telling it. I had an image of a little bear drawn to create a visual for the Bearhunt brand.

Then, as I told the story and sent things out, did things with people and got some paying clients, amazingly, the ball began to roll in a way that I had not expected.

First I found that the metaphor of the family overcoming obstacles and busting through them, rather than tinkering around at the edges, was something that people readily identified with. Without producing a brochure, mission statement, strategy document or any of the other paraphernalia, people just seemed to get it. From this simple story, they got what I was about. They had made a connection at an intellectual level, without any hard sell, and people began to stick.

After a while I noticed how often, particularly when talking to senior managers in the public sector, people wanted to veer off from the discussion of their obstacles to talk about the story itself. They had their own specific memories of sitting on the edge of the bed reading to their children.

As they talked, you could almost see them replaying the image in their minds. For parents, this is perhaps the most magical time of their lives: when their children are young and entranced by the story you are telling them. The story *We're Going on a Bear Hunt* has a particular chorus at the end of each page – 'We can't go under it. We can't go over it. We'll have to go through it' – and many parents recalled the wonderful feeling of calling this out in unison with their children. It invokes memories of connection, of family, of life at its best.

So I began to realize that people not only identified intellectually with these simple few lines that I had written to describe what I was about – they identified emotionally.

It often means that I have established an intellectual and emotional connection even before I have walked through the door, because I am then able to talk with conviction and passion, I believe what I am about, and I'm not pretending or delivering a sales pitch. People seem to stick.

And then, of course, there are the women. It had never crossed my mind before, but women in particular seem to form some deep emotional attachment to bears. This kind of stickiness started in the very early days of Bearhunt. My PA left a scribbled note on my desk, a message from a lady I had never heard of that said 'Tell Malcolm I love him.' I got rather excited by this and immediately returned the call. The 'him' she was referring to was the little hand-drawn bear that I had produced to go on my letterhead.

It didn't stop there. I regularly receive e-mails, phone calls and handwritten notes from ladies who want to talk about the bear. It's great; it's sticky. They never forget me and what I do, and best of all they tell other people.

Recently, I was involved in a competitive pitch for a large-scale piece of work spanning four years. One of the team assessing more than 30 proposals told me how he had taken them home to read through over the weekend. He laid them all out on the kitchen table.

As his girlfriend walked by, she pointed to my bear image and said 'That's the winner.' As it happens, she was right. I'm sure she was just attracted to the bear rather than having any intuitive insight, but it just reinforces my belief that this thing has stickiness.

I wish that I could claim that getting this intellectual and emotional buy-in – as well as bear-loving groupies – was a stroke of genius. In truth, I don't think it was. I just tried to write something that was different and engaging, truly said what I was about, and that I enjoyed telling and re-telling.

It has become a sticky ball, and it's been amazing to watch how sticky balls pick up momentum.

Whether you want to be a florist, an artist, a restaurateur, a wrestler, a clown, or whatever, you will need to create your own sticky ball. Just as Andrew Mawson has done, and just as I've done, you can do it through stories that create connection and invoke strong mental images and feelings that people want to attach themselves to.

You will need to develop your storytelling skills.

The power of stories

Throughout history, people have memorized and relayed their experiences and concerns through stories.

Great orators such as Martin Luther King and Winston Churchill seem to have a gift for it, and there's no doubt about it: they were truly brilliant.

They instinctively understood the ingredients of a great speech, a great story and a great delivery. They could paint pictures with words. Churchill may have seemed a natural, but his performance was well-rehearsed. He would spend hours working and reworking important speeches, changing a word here, inserting a pause there, to achieve just the right dramatic effect.

All of us can tell stories. Sometimes we tell them better than at other times. When we are really passionate about something, we seem to throw away the script and talk from the heart.

To create your sticky ball, you must create a story that resonates with all the passion that you feel about doing what you love. There are a number of elements which make up great stories. They are listed below.

Relate, relate, relate

People respond to things that they can relate to. The bear hunt story is a good example, where people can relate to it intellectually and emotionally. Think about the people you are talking to. Try to get into their shoes and understand what they might relate to.

Give it oomph

Make your stories powerful using some or all of these methods:

- Re-experience the event. A good way to do this is to talk in the present tense. Notice how often Andrew Mawson does this. He talks about his meeting with doctors at The Royal London Hospital in this way: *'Then of course it all begins to crack open and you get two hours of who's not spoken to whom. I just sit and watch, and it was like spaghetti all over the table. The truth was coming out.'*
- Use descriptive sensory language: *'I'm in my little vestry in an empty church and this guy walks in with a face that looks like a sculpture, but a sculpture that's been to Hell and back. I began to listen …'*
- Be succinct. Dare to use a few words to get a point over: *'Answer: "Because your fax number had changed."'*
- Emphasize emotional content: *'I said, "I've had enough of this conversation. It is all about you guys protecting your backs. It's not about Jean Viles, who was the customer. If you ran a business like this you would be bankrupt in three weeks."'*
- Be prepared to play different roles in the story: *'And yes, Andrew, I polish it every Thursday.'*
- Vary your vocal style and use your body to reinforce points: empathize, relax, and so on.

Do be personal

Stories from our own lives often contain universal themes, with experiences or situations that other people have been through too. If we can make them relevant, the chances are that people will relate to them.

Have a point

A good story is not enough. It has to have a point. You are telling the story so that people will take away its message and create a belief. Make sure that you convey your point unambiguously.

Everyone loves a good story

With a great story, told well, who needs visual aids? I recently heard a radio programme that imagined how things might have been if *PowerPoint*, Microsoft's presentational software, had been around in Winston Churchill's day.
It went something like this:

Er, right. Let's have a look at the first slide here. Oh yes, the timetable. Well, as you can see, we will go on to the end. If I just flip over to the next one ... you'll see the areas we will operate in. Er, seas, oceans, beaches ... landing grounds. Oh yes, even streets, and – er – a little bit on the hills. Oh yes, last slide. We are not going to surrender. Er – so that's about it, really. Thank you.

Thankfully, Churchill made his broadcast over the radio waves and had to create the image in the minds of the nation ...

We shall go on to the end, we shall fight in France, we shall fight on the seas and oceans, we shall fight with growing confidence and growing strength in the air, we shall defend our island, whatever the cost may be, we shall fight on the beaches, we shall fight on the landing grounds, we shall fight in the fields and in the streets, we shall fight in the hills; we shall never surrender, and even if, which I do not for a moment believe, this Island or a large part of it were subjugated and starving, then our Empire beyond the seas, armed and guarded by the British Fleet, would carry on the struggle, until, in God's good time, the New World, with all its power and might, steps forth to the rescue and the liberation of the old.

To earn your living doing what you love, you will need your own sticky ball. It will start from a great story. Get good at telling great stories, and remember: when you are really passionate about what you do, it will all come naturally. Use the tips here to refine and develop your story and have maximum, unforgettable impact.

The power of connection and Gladwell's Law of the Few

Having a great story is one thing; working out who to tell it to and how to tell it is an art and a science – something worth paying attention to. It is yet another one of those situations where micro inputs can have macro outputs and where small things can make a big difference.

Quite often I am invited to attend 'networking events'. Usually the invitation says 'bring plenty of business cards with you'.

Part of me says I ought to go. When you get to Chapter 5 ('Luck be a lady tonight – applying the science of luck'), you will wonder why I don't go. One of the key factors of luck is to create chance opportunities – and meeting lots of people is always a chance opportunity.

Connection is truly a powerful force. To achieve real power from connection, it is important to understand better the significance of relationships and Gladwell's Law of the Few.

Once you understand these things, it becomes clear that there are better, more effective, more rewarding ways of building connections than handing out business cards like a trackside bookmaker on speed.

We are all different – some people are more different than others

If everybody were the same, and information passed between people at an even rate and in the same way, then handing out business cards by the bucketload would be as good a strategy as any.

However, there are many different types of people. It is people who are responsible for the passage of ideas, trends, movements and behavioural norms, and the way that they spread through society. Malcolm Gladwell's bestseller *The Tipping Point* likens this diffusion process to the way epidemics spread. One moment the prevalence of 'flu is going along quite steadily at an even pace, then suddenly, almost in an instant, it can take hold of a population and grow like wildfire.

The technical term for 'growing like wildfire' is geometrical progression or exponential growth; that is, growth so rapid that it is hard for our minds to grasp at first. To explain the power of such growth, you have to imagine taking a piece of paper. Fold it over, then fold it over again. If you were able to fold it

50 times, how high do you think the stack would be? When I ask people this question, some will say 'as thick as a telephone directory'. Others may feel bold enough to say 'as high as a table'. The official answer, according to Gladwell, is that the stack would reach as far as the sun.

I would be surprised if you were not surprised. In fact, so many people have ridiculed me for believing this, that I created a simple mathematical model using a spreadsheet. After three turns of the paper, it is as thick as a fingernail. It takes seven turns before it is as thick as a notebook. By the fourteenth turn, it is 1.6 metres high. That's as tall as an adult. Doubling and doubling again, by the thirtieth turn it will have reached the outer limits of the atmosphere. Now the doubling effect goes crazy so that at the fiftieth turn, your stack of paper is 112,589,990,684 metres high. That's about 95 million miles – the distance to the sun. Just one more fold, of course, will take you to the sun and back.

According to Gladwell, ideas and trends spread in the same way that epidemics do, reaching a 'tipping point', and we just have to understand what makes them tip. How do we get to a situation where at one moment our idea is bobbing along, then suddenly, all Hell breaks loose.

We have to understand the 'power of the few'.

Gladwell's Law of the Few

I think this is the reason that I don't attend too many networking events. These events are more like the 'impotence of the many', which, when compared with the 'power of the few' is a less attractive yet easier proposition.

I say it is easier, because it is: you walk into a room, sound off about your idea like a double glazing salesman on speed, hand out your business cards and feel that you have done a good night's work.

But will your idea really spread like an epidemic? Possibly, but only if:

- the room is populated with three different types of people;
- you understood the way each of them operates;
- you understood the critical nature of their interactions;
- you had a story that had stickiness; and
- you understood the power of context.

You can imagine that this is much harder than simply attending a networking event and handing out cards willy-nilly. Typically, a networking event will have an impact related to cause and effect – the return you get out, the spread of your idea, will roughly relate to cause and effect. You will get a return roughly equivalent to the effort you put in. It will be harder to assess how to spread your idea as if it were an epidemic, but if you can do it, in just 50 turns of a page, you can go to the sun – and back. You can make your idea spread like wildfire.

There are three types of people that contribute to creating a word-of-mouth epidemic, which is how you want your idea to spread. Whether it is about you, your business or your product, you want it to spread like a virus.

So what kind of people are we looking for? When I tell you, it will not come as a surprise; you will most likely be able to identify these types quite readily. They are, in Gladwell's terms, Connectors, Mavens and Salespeople.

It's a gift

Why do some ideas tip and others don't? A big part of the success of a social epidemic can be attributed to the involvement of people with a particular gift for bringing the world together: the Connectors.

If you make a list of your 40 closest friends, excluding family and work colleagues, then work backwards through the chain of events that led to your friendship. You will most likely find that ultimately, almost all of them came about as a direct or indirect result of your friendship with one or two people.

These people, the Connectors, join up our world and join our world with the worlds of others. They are the people that seem to know everyone. It is not just that they know a lot of people – it is the nature of their relationships that is important. They tend to be 'masters of the weak tie'. In other words, they maintain lots and lots of friendly, yet casual, relationships. Whereas many of us have some close friends and acquaintances, Connectors are habitually adding more friendly, casual relationships to their portfolio.

This is important in spreading a social epidemic. Of course if you know lots of people, then you can pass on information to lots of people. Yet the nature of a Connector's relationships is important too. We tend to know much the same information and gossip as our close friends; Connectors pass on information to acquaintances, so it tends to be *new* information, and they in turn pass on that information within their social circle.

Imagine now that you have a new idea, or say you are opening a restaurant, and you want to spread the word. If you tell a Connector and they tell 40 people, 2 of the 40 may be Connectors. If the message is sticky enough, they may each tell 40 people, and amongst them may be more Connectors.

The effect is slow at first, but just like the piece of paper, within 50 folds it will make a very, very big number. An epidemic will be on the march, thanks to the gifted, gregarious, extrovert Connectors who join our world together.

Everyone knows a Maven

In the Yiddish, 'Maven' means 'one who accumulates knowledge'. In the world of social epidemics, where ideas and trends spread through word of mouth, the Maven is a very important person.

You could assert that Connectors, because they know lots of people, learn about new information by a random process. According to Gladwell, though, if you look at social epidemics, there are people that we rely on to connect us to new information. Just as Connectors are people specialists, Mavens are information specialists.

We all know a Maven. These are the people that take an extraordinarily detailed interest in a particular area. For instance, I can count in my circle a restaurant Maven; a hotel Maven; a social policy Maven. When I was younger. one of my friends had an encyclopaedic knowledge of film. Not only did he know the stars and the plots, he could also quote dialogue, tell you who the sound engineer was and what they had worked on before. He would tell you which cinema had the most comfortable seats, why you should go at a particular time, whereabouts you should sit, the price of a hotdog and so on.

It is this almost obsessive attention to detail that marks out the Maven. They speak with authority and are noted for their knowledge. When they pass on new knowledge, such as an opinion on a new restaurant, people place a great deal of faith in the opinion. There is also something about the motivation of the Maven: their joy tends to come from sharing their information with others. It is not just self-conscious 'plugging'; a message that is personal, without self-interest and expert tends to make us take notice.

You can imagine what happens when a Maven passes information to a Connector. The power of the message is also interesting. When a connector tells twenty people to stay in a particular hotel, seven of them might do it. If a Maven tells five people to stay in the same hotel, it is likely that all five will follow the advice. That is the power of the Maven.

The Persuaders

Mavens give a message authority and spread it to a few. Connectors are promiscuous with knowledge and spread it to many. Between them, they are the data bank and the glue.

There is another type of person who is important in making a social epidemic tip. These are the persuaders – the Salespeople. These are the people who have a particular set of skills to persuade us about an idea when we are unconvinced of what we are hearing.

They have energy, enthusiasm, charm and likeability. They can help us create a message that is irresistible to Mavens and Connectors, and the people that they come into contact with.

The significance of relationships

You can write business plans until you are blue in the face. You change the figures and change the assumptions until the numbers add up to the numbers you want to see.

What really matters in terms of earning your living by doing what you love is how you go about building connections. Andrew Mawson's approach in Bromley by Bow was to create more and more connections between people and ideas. Stories began to emerge and they created a sticky ball that more and more people stuck to as it rolled.

You don't necessarily have to be the world's most gregarious person to capitalize upon the immense power of connection. You simply have to create a great story and identify the Connectors, Mavens and Salespeople in your particular world. Your work is then about experimenting with different ways to get the story flowing and to increase its intensity and credibility.

This is important work that has no beginning – because even now you have already spent time talking to these kind of people – and no end. The world does not stand still and there will be new ideas, Mavens will come and go, new Connectors will emerge and different kinds of Salespeople will be needed at different times.

It will be work that is worthwhile. It will save you a fortune in advertising, mail-shots and business cards, but it is unlikely to save you time. Building relationships and developing your story should constantly be in your thoughts. If you persevere, it will be immensely rewarding and satisfying.

If you think of it in these terms, whatever your idea, just 51 turns of the page could take you to the sun – and back.

5

Luck be a lady tonight – applying the science of luck

The 'Iron Chancellor', Gordon Brown, rose to his feet to address an invited audience at the Treasury. The subject was the future of Britain's childcare and 'early years' policy. He had assembled the country's movers and shakers to get them to embrace new ideas.

For support he had, to his left, ministerial colleague Margaret Hodge. On his right was Phillip Collins – a man with a smile on his face.

As he surveyed the audience, Collins realized that all of them had probably been in childcare for at least 20 years. He had been thinking about these issues for less than six months, yet the Chancellor wanted them to listen to his ideas.

Collins was loving it. He had a smile on his face, even though he had taken a pay cut of about £200,000 a year to do it. Yes – he was doing what he loved.

Some people might say it was a stroke of bad luck, to lose a job that paid £250,000 a year. But Philip Collins didn't lose it. He was a rising star in the world of investment banking – he just walked out and made his own luck.

He is highly intelligent, young and good-looking, he had a great career, and he was wealthy. He had the world at his feet. Yet his life lacked something – something that was immensely important to him. Passion.

I worked in financial services for a few years. I was in the City as an investment banker. I didn't ever love it. I really enjoyed it for a while and then I began to hate it. I began to be there just because the money was good. I packed it in simply because I couldn't bear doing something I didn't like. I think I'm unusual in that my threshold for doing things I don't like is very low, and I'm lucky in that I was able to move into something I like.

I was lucky in that I had the brainpower, the contacts and also the attitude to risk that allowed me to do it. I took a pay cut of 80%. Now not many people are prepared to do that. I went from £250,000 a year to £25,000 at first. I was bored. Not many people are prepared to do that. Lots of people who do high-powered jobs but don't enjoy them are making a trade-off so that things that they do enjoy are paid for by the things that they don't. It's probably more complex than that – they are doing things that they love, but they are paid for by their job.

I know a lot of good friends who have made this point to me many times. They are clever, intelligent, rounded people who are doing something quite dull in the City. They admit that they find it a bit one-dimensional, but they really enjoy the lifestyle that they have. They are doing lots of things that they love, but not at work.

They make a stronger split between their work life and their home life, which I've never been able to do, really.

Despite the substantial income, Collins himself couldn't summon up enough love for the job.

City jobs can be quite one-dimensional, but mine, in City terms wasn't like that.

I was an equity strategist. I had to translate the views of the Chief Economist into what an investor should do in the market. I just wasn't that interested in financial markets in the end. Lots of people are. There are some people who love that job, but I wasn't one of them.

If you are good, you will earn the bank a commission of 0.2% on every trade that they do. They would probably earn £15 million off my labour for that year, so the question might be, why do they pay you so little? Why are they exploiting you so much? The surplus on your labour is massive.

There's a bit of a 'star' system, so it's a bit like, why do Premier League footballers get paid so much? There's a kind of a scarcity value on them because there are so few of them, and the group of really good traders in the City is fairly small.

It's interpretation. It's showbusiness. Not so much analysis: there are some people who think it's all about the analysis, but they're wrong. The thing that marks out someone who is good from someone who is OK at it is not the quality of their analysis, it's whether they can make sales on it.

Because it's selling, really, but what you are selling is ideas. You are trying to persuade an investor to invest in an idea that you're offering them. It's intellectual salesmanship, but in the end it's business – showbusiness. So if you are a good impresario, then that's worth more than if you are just a quiet person who is analytical.

Really good teams have someone who is quiet back at the office doing really hard number-crunching with good quality work. Then you need someone who goes out there and sells it.

He quite clearly recalls the incident that made up his mind that he wanted to pursue a different kind of life.

There was one day when I was sitting there and the issue being discussed in the office – a big deal for us – was which of the indices was going to be the big one in the future, would it be the German DAX or the French CAC, and I thought, I couldn't begin to care about this. I just couldn't begin to. I just said something really bitter and twisted about how boring this whole thing was and everyone kind of noticed. Someone said, 'You hate this, don't you?' And I said, 'Yes. It's absolutely dire.'

I sort of knew then, but I must admit the day that I resigned, I went into work not intending to resign. I'd sort of decided that at some point I might leave because it was so awful, but I hadn't intended to leave on that day. It just came up in a meeting with my boss and I thought, 'Oh, I might as well resign.' I had nothing to go to.

I left at the worst possible moment because I'd just started to rake it in, because I'd had a massive pay rise. I had a reasonable amount put by – enough to tide me over for a few months while I wrote a novel, but after three or four months I was desperately in need of a job.

Collins eventually joined the Social Market Foundation, an independent think tank providing a source of innovative economic and social policy ideas. It tries to influence government and policy-makers in health, education, welfare and pensions policy reform.

Essentially, I run a small business. The output of our business is pamphlets, ideas, seminars and policy discussions. So that involves me in a massive range of subjects. I'm the spokesman, I do a lot of journalism, it's about five jobs in one, which is what I like about it. I do lots of punditry on the TV and radio, I do lots of public speaking, which I really enjoy, I do quite a lot of writing and editing, I manage twelve people and the budget and I do a lot of fundraising. So you have to be part entrepreneur, part journalist, part academic and part businessman. I quite like all of that because I get bored just doing one of them.

I'm now in charge of the place, which I wasn't when I moved, so the gap between my current salary and my City salary has closed a bit – not that much, but a bit.

He can talk with great enthusiasm about the things he's done since he left investment banking, but does he have any regrets?

I've written two novels, which I'm really proud of – one of them was a bestseller. That was great. At work there have been a couple of publications which I'm proud of. We've done a lot of work on childcare and policy for the early years of life, and I was invited to speak at the Treasury. The three speakers were Gordon Brown, Margaret Hodge and me, and the audience comprised people who had been working in this field for 20 years. Six months after starting it we were up there at the top table presenting our thoughts on what should happen and that was fantastic.

That's when think tanks really work well: jumping into a topic and leapfrogging and making a real difference. I was very proud of that.

The ideas are much more interesting. I care about the ideas intrinsically. I have genuine views about policy for childcare and it matters to me in a way that I don't have genuine views about whether brewers are going to outperform the food manufacturing companies, and I don't care either way.

Whereas when I'm talking about, say, public service reform, I'm not just making it up. It means something to me and that's why I enjoy it.

No regrets. Never. Absolutely never, because I enjoy what I do now so much more. It just engages me, my brain, so much more. It's different everyday and I have a really good job.

This is a remarkably upbeat assessment from someone who walked out on a salary beyond the wildest dreams of most people and into the unknown, unaware of how he would earn a living. One of the reasons he was able to do it was his attitude: he has an attitude that cultivates luck.

I do have a sort of faith that it will be OK – I do have an idea in my mind that everything will be just fine and there's no need to worry. I don't worry about things at all. I worry so little that people around me worry that I don't worry enough.

You make your own luck, in a way. I don't know why I believe this, because I don't believe in any of those things like fate or destiny. I just think things will be okay. I suppose I've got faith in my own ability, so that if things should take a turn for the worse, I'll find something else to do. I'm just phlegmatic; not prone to brooding on things or worrying about things.

I shut things out quite well and just deal with it. I've got a peculiar mixture of being ambitious and not being ambitious. I'm ambitious but I don't know what for. There's nothing in particular that I desperately want to do all the time. I'm relentlessly unfocused. I love being off the curriculum.

Phillip Collins is lucky because he thinks lucky. If you want to earn your living by doing what you love, as Phillip Collins does, you will have to learn to cultivate your luck.

Impossible, some may say. You are either lucky or unlucky – that's that.

Not so. You can increase your luck, and there is firm scientific evidence to help you to work out how. So, let's be like Phillip Collins and get lucky.

The science of luck

Lucky people have an uncanny knack of being in the right place at the right time.

If this does not seem to be an apt description of you, then it is time that you began to think about and practice the science of luck. Even if you are an exceptionally lucky person, you can still improve your good fortune.

I have always led what I regard to be a charmed life, with chance meetings, small insights, serendipity and helpful people nudging me along just at the right moment. When I stumbled across the science of luck, I began to understand why.

Then I noticed something. During short spells in my life when I have not been quite as lucky, I had neglected the four principles of luck. I then wrote them out and took to looking at them every day. I tried to be much more *consistent* in my approach to achieving good fortune. I was absolutely amazed at the impact that it had on all aspects of my life.

You can call it coincidence if you like. Or you can understand the principles of luck and see what happens when you apply them *consistently*.

Professor Richard Wiseman now heads up an academic research unit at the University of Hertfordshire. Before that he was a magician, and it was his interest in illusion that got him thinking about what goes on inside people's heads. He went to university and gained a doctorate in psychology.

He has always majored on psychological phenomena – the unexplained – and was often asked to give talks on his work. He would introduce these talks using a simple magic trick. He would borrow a £10 note from a member of the audience, place it into one of 20 identical envelopes and then mix them up. He would then ask the person to select one envelope. The rest he would set fire to.

Whilst performing this trick one evening, he stumbled across a theme that would take him into a new unchartered area of research – luck.

He had kept track of the envelope with the money in and was delighted when the woman selected it. He than set fire to the other 19 envelopes, and duly gave the woman her £10 note. The audience cheered and applauded as usual, but the woman remained deadpan.

When he asked if she was surprised that she got her money back, she was quite matter-of-fact, saying that this kind of thing happened to her all the time. She couldn't explain why, she just put it down to being lucky.

Other people in the audience had similar views. Others still had quite the opposite views. Their lives were filled with misfortune. Why?

In his book *The Luck Factor*, Wiseman distils the findings from working with hundreds of people over eight years of research to try to determine what makes some people lucky and others unlucky.

He has uncovered four principles. People who are lucky are not lucky because they work exceptionally hard, are amazingly talented or exceptionally intelligent; the four principles that they use are all about behaviour and attitude. The great news is that you can learn them and adapt your behaviour.

Even if you are very lucky, the chances are you could become even luckier. Let's take a look at Wiseman's four principles in the context of earning your living by doing what you love.

Principle one: maximize your chance opportunities

It was Chris Joyce, the former Simply Red drummer and partner in Manchester's Love Saves The Day urban convenience store, who summed it up:

> You create your own luck. You've got to be out and about and doing things for things to happen. If you are sitting down in your living room, waiting for things to happen, they won't. You've got to create your own luck.

That's what this principle is about. Lucky people tend not to sit in their living room waiting. They create, notice and act upon the chance opportunities in their life. They tend to be more extrovert, meet more people, try more things and are relaxed enough to notice opportunity.

Build and maintain a strong network of luck

Extroverts are better at doing this than introverts, so the more you can cultivate your outward behaviour – going out and talking to people – the better.

Meeting lots of people is the same principle as buying a lottery ticket: 'you have to be in it to win it'. By being out there, lucky people dramatically increase their chances of having a chance encounter. By meeting a great number of people, they increase their potential to run into someone that has a positive effect on their lives.

Andrew Mawson, when he took over the dilapidated church in Bromley by Bow took the unusual step of allowing sculptor Santiago Bell to build a workshop in the church. Activities in and around the church exploded when he clarified the philosophy:

> Janet arrived with this idea of developing a dance school and we said yes. Santiago and a few of us said, 'Why not just say yes to everybody? What have you got to lose?'

He was, in effect, creating a climate where chance opportunity could grow exponentially. A crumbling church with £400 in the bank grew to become a centre with a £2 million turnover and create more than 100 jobs. I guess he just got lucky.

Gerald Epstein was going to remain at his apartment in Jerusalem whilst his wife went to interview an old Algerian woman.

> I didn't want to go because I had sat in these interviews and they were quite boring. But a voice came from somewhere and said, 'Go'. It was an imperative 'Go'.
> So I followed it I went outside and said 'Wait, I'm coming with you.'

He created a chance opportunity, and so he met Madame Collete Aboulker-Muscat. She introduced him to the concept of the 'waking dream' and it transformed his life.

A young Gavin Cargill was making nearly twice his salary through commissions on life policies sold to people he had introduced to an agent than he made as a bank clerk. He could have stayed at home and counted the money. Instead:

'I thought, 'Well, that's interesting.' So I asked my agent, how do I do your job?

His agent created a chance opportunity and introduced him to the boss in Edinburgh. Given his own territory, Cargill became Britain's number two top-selling financial services advisor. It began by making a chance opportunity.

Another way that people increase the number of chance encounters they have is to become a social magnet. Extroverts, in particular, seem to be able to draw other people towards them. Social magnets show the types of body language and facial expressions that other people find attractive and inviting. Wiseman's work with people who believe that they are lucky shows that they exhibit the same sort of characteristics.

Perhaps the most important aspect of creating chance opportunities is summed up again by Andrew Mawson, as the church began to develop ideas for a nursery:

We began to do it and a group of relationships began to happen.

Lucky people are good at building secure and long-lasting relationships with the people that they meet; they are not 'here today, gone tomorrow'. They are easy to get to know and other people tend to like them, they show trust, and they form close rather than superficial relationships.

So to increase your chance opportunities you must get out there; you must be open and social; and create secure, long-lasting relationships that have to be about much more than 'what's in it for me?'.

Have a relaxed attitude towards life

Wiseman has found that lucky people tend to spot opportunities better because they are calm and relaxed. In his study of lucky and unlucky people he found that the unlucky group tended to have a much higher score on his measure of 'neuroticism'. They were much more tense and anxious than the lucky people.

It's not that lucky people necessarily expect to find chance opportunities, but their relaxed way of looking at the world increases their ability to notice them. Anxious people have a very narrow, focused beam of attention that can cause them to miss all of those unexpected opportunities that surround them every day.

Perhaps this is how Phillip Collins was able to resign from his £250,000-a-year job as an investment banker without knowing what he was going to do.

> I don't worry about things at all. I worry so little that people around me worry that I don't worry enough.

Lucky people don't go to parties trying hard to find their dream mate or to networking events to drum up business. They just relax and therefore become more attuned to the opportunities around them. They listen and just see what is there rather than trying to find what they want to see.

Open yourself to new experiences

A lot depends on whether your approach to life is conventional or unconventional. Lucky people have a high score on an index that Wiseman calls 'openness'.

They will try new things, taste new foods, go to different places. They like variety and novelty. Rather than being bound by convention, they like the notion of unpredictability.

Again, Phillip Collins shows himself to be lucky in this respect:

> I'm relentlessly unfocused. I love being off the curriculum.

Andrew Mawson kept coming up against people who weren't open to new experiences. The first time was when the officers from Social Services came to visit:

> 'You can't possibly have a church and a nursery because there's all these rules and regulations.' She put her hand in her bag and pulled out the encyclopaedia of a thousand reasons why it couldn't be done.

It happened again when his team saw a chance opportunity to create a new kind of integrated health centre:

The senior health people looked at me as if I had said we were going to build a nuclear weapons site in the park.

The mindset was 'we run health'. Instead of them coming back with nine other ideas, it was all about 'we must stop this', not 'we must build something'. It was, 'We must stop this because we are in power, we are in charge.'

Only Andrew's persistence and willingness to defy convention made something happen.

Principle two: listen to your lucky hunches

How often in the stories in this book have we heard about this? In the chapters that follow, you will hear more of it. Lucky people make successful decisions by using their intuition and gut feelings.

When Wiseman looked at the difference between lucky and unlucky people in terms of their intuitive abilities, he said that 'the results were to show the remarkable abilities of our unconscious minds.' If you remember, this is a proposition that Dr Gerald Epstein would agree with.

Wiseman again surveyed lucky and unlucky people to look at how people used their intuition to make important life decisions – careers, personal relationships, business and finance. He found that lucky people used intuition much more in all four areas.

Psychologists have shown repeatedly that our unconscious retains information and, although we cannot always consciously remember it, it is used as a prompt during our everyday lives. Sometimes when we are introduced to someone new we have a feeling about them. It can be either positive or negative, but we can't quite put our finger on why. Experiments suggest that these intuitive impressions depend on the hidden workings of our unconscious mind. Some people ignore these feelings; others take notice of them and use them as part of the mix when it comes to making important life decisions.

Wiseman gives a good example:

We all have wants and desires. Most people would like to find their perfect partner or discover an easy way of making lots of money. For some people, these desires can exert a powerful influence over how they view the world, and can even cause them to see what they want to see rather than what is actually right in front of their noses. The desire to find the perfect partner might make them overlook obvious signs of deceit or incompatibility. Their need to make easy money might cause them to invest in an obvious scam or confidence game. However, unconsciously, these people often realize that they are deceiving themselves into believing what they want to believe. Deep down, they know something is wrong, and often this rather odd feeling emerges as a kind of intuition – an inner voice or a gut feeling telling them that they are kidding themselves. Some people listen to this inner voice and others choose to continue their wishful thinking and self-denial.

Despite the advice of a number of accountants, Chris Joyce created Love Saves The Day when he decided he was going to back his intuition:

The accountants were all very negative about it. It's when you get so far down the line with something, there's no pulling back no matter what advice people give you. You just think, 'We had our instincts of how we wanted to carry on.'

Throughout his life, Andrew Mawson has always backed his intuition.

There are moments. My instinct was telling me that the moment was right. It wasn't though out of some business plan or some clever analytical document, it was just me following my instinct. Over the years my instinct, about 90% of the time, has turned out to be a fairly reliable guide.

Now that he is building up a network of 'social entrepreneurs' across the country, I once asked him how I would recognize one of these if I bumped into one. His answer confirms his intuitive nature.

You just know, Malcolm. You know within two minutes of meeting them – they've got something.

Boost your intuition

Wiseman went back to his group of lucky and unlucky people to see if they did anything to boost their intuition. Again, there were marked differences: lucky people engaged in more intuition-boosting activities than the unlucky group. These were meditation, returning to the problem later, clearing the mind and finding a quiet place.

Perhaps it was just coincidence, but Dr Gerald Epstein had been undergoing a course of meditation in Jerusalem immediately prior to having that irresistible feeling that he should accompany his wife on her visit to see Madame Collete Aboulker-Muscat.

As you contemplate earning your living by doing what you love, take steps to boost your intuition and listen more carefully to the feelings you have.

Principle three: expect good fortune

When asked to rate the chances of a range of positive and negative events happening, Wiseman was astounded at the differences between lucky and unlucky people.

On all the positive events, the lucky people scored higher: they believed that there was a good chance of good things happening. On all the negative events, unlucky people scored higher: they had a belief that bad things were going to happen to them.

These sorts of expectations have a powerful impact on our lives. They affect the way we feel and therefore the way we act. These thoughts enable lucky people to be more effective than most when it comes to achieving their dreams and ambitions. The unlucky expectations of the unlucky people often mean that they don't even try.

In this way we create self-fulfilling prophesies that we are either lucky or unlucky. This relates closely to Dr Gerald Epstein's point when he compared his old life of psychoanalysis with his new life of mental imagery.

Epstein now disputes the traditional Freudian approach that 'what I experience creates what I believe'. He says, 'This is what I was labouring with under Freud – the experiences of my childhood determine what I become like as an adult. In other words, my experience becomes my reality.' This is clearly the viewpoint of the unlucky people.

And the lucky people seem to adopt the same approach as Epstein's imagery school of thought: 'We are saying, "No – what I believe becomes my experience and my reality".'

You are what you believe you are.

Start to create good fortune by creating images of good fortune in your mind.

Perseverance and tenacity

These self-fulfilling prophesies affect the way that people, lucky and unlucky, go about pursuing daily tasks and long-term goals.

The negative beliefs of the unlucky can cause them to quickly lose hope and quickly give up.

When Wiseman showed his two groups two metal puzzles with interlocking parts, he told them that one could be solved and one was impossible to solve. With each person he tossed a coin to see which puzzle they should examine. He handed them one of the puzzles and asked them to see if they thought it was possible or impossible.

Over 60% of the unlucky people said that the puzzle was impossible, compared with 30% of the lucky people. In fact, he handed everyone the same puzzle. Again, the unlucky people had effectively given up before they had even started.

Lucky people also tend to persevere at something much more even if their chances of achieving it are slim, because they expect things to work out, they carry on towards achieving their goals.

Many people would have thrown in the towel had their business not made a profit in its first four years, but not Chris Joyce of Love Saves The Day:

> The first four years were extremely difficult because we didn't know what we were doing. It was passion that drove us for those first four years, because it certainly wasn't bloody money. It cost me money for those first four years.

Or Andrew Mawson in Bromley by Bow, who continued to cajole a resistant Health Authority for support in building a health centre. He would not give up and after three years the Health Minister Dr Brian Mawhinney intervened.

Or Dr Gerald Epstein who was ostracized by his colleagues for flying in the face of the analytical tradition:

> I lost everything. I became destitute financially. I had to take a job in a clinic monitoring people who had been put on medication.
>
> I lost my income, I lost my friends, my family thought I had gone crazy, my wife was under a great deal of tension about the shift that I had made so abruptly without discussing it with her – I felt like I was choked. I would have lost my home had I not got this job. It was this job that allowed me to continue living and paying rent. We scrimped along. We just managed.

He believed in good fortune:

Faith. Why would I give everything up and trade it in at that moment after an inspirational thought? I had faith in her. I went through an experience which was indescribable by words. I had faith in her and what she was going to teach me.

Expect your interactions with others to be lucky

This self-fulfilling prophesy about luck also seems to affect the interactions that lucky people have with others. They expect their interactions to go well, so they tend to be positive, to smile and to initiate an upbeat conversation.

This tends to trigger a similar response in the other person, and a virtuous cycle begins that increases the probability of a successful interaction.

Gavin Cargill became Britain's number two financial services advisor not because he went and frightened people about the need for life insurance or bored them with the technicalities of insurance underwriting. He went to have a positive interaction with them and revelled in the joy of telling them interesting stories. He consistently had positive interactions and people wanted to buy from him.

Principle four: turn bad luck into good

Lucky people have ill fortune sometimes too, but what is interesting is how they handle it. They have an uncanny knack of transforming their misfortune into amazing good luck. Lucky people have 'bouncebackability'.

Lucky people, when faced with unlucky scenarios, consistently looked on the bright side of a situation, spontaneously imagining how things could have been worse. This helped them to maintain the notion that they were lucky people living lucky lives.

Ill fortune will in the long run work out for the best

Very often, when you look back on your life, you can find two or three things that would not have happened if you had not experienced a particular misfortune. Divorce is an unfortunate and painful experience that many people have to endure. For many, it is traumatic; but so often in the long run, good luck comes out of bad. You may have children; you have learned a lot about how relationships do and don't work; you can more accurately assess what you want in a new relationship; you have more freedom and an opportunity to try new experiences; you may even find the love of your life.

Lucky people tend to anticipate a positive long-term benefit when faced with an immediate misfortune.

Don't dwell – take constructive steps

Also, lucky people tend not to dwell on ill-fortune. They are good at just letting go of the past and getting on with the future. Conversely, unlucky people will ruminate upon a bad situation, sometimes even creating a myth about a 'curse' or a 'jinx' that only serves to sustain their belief in bad luck. They focus upon finding incidents that support the 'jinx' theory.

In addition to not dwelling, lucky people take positive steps to avoid similar misfortune in the future. They develop risk management strategies by simply looking at what went wrong, why, and what *they* can do to prevent it from happening again.

Now get lucky

When you earn your living by doing what you love, you have to have a lot of luck in all facets of you life. The great thing is that this rules no-one out: we all have great potential to be lucky. All we have to do is apply Wiseman's four principles every day.

To do that, you don't have to be exceptionally intelligent, gifted or privileged; you simply have to pay attention to your attitudes and behaviours, and do it consistently – every day.

I realize that I have been able to do what I love because I have been lucky. I can now see that I am one of the people who throughout my life have applied Wiseman's principles quite well.

I now concentrate much more on applying them well and *consistently*, and I have been astounded at the impact that consistency has on an already lucky life.

This book was written because I made a conscious effort to apply the principles of luck to make it happen and find a publisher. It was completed because bad luck was turned into good. My co-author rang the week before Christmas to say that she was pulling out. I could have thrown in the towel.

Instead, I immediately found five reasons why her pulling out was a remarkable stroke of luck. I realized that I had to focus massively over the festive period if I was to create even more good luck out of bad. After five days, I had written 26,000 words. I learned things about myself: just how focused, resilient and disciplined I could be when I wanted to be, and how much I enjoyed writing – yet more good luck coming out of bad.

You need no qualifications to be lucky; you just have to start to apply the principles every day. You might want to keep a notebook handy so that each day, you can document what happens when you apply the principles to your life. This way you will reinforce the behaviours and in time become increasingly lucky.

So what are you waiting for? Go and get lucky.

6

Develop your millionaire mind

Edstone Hall is a rambling country pile in the picturesque market town of Henley-in-Arden in Warwickshire. This peaceful, rural haven seemed an unlikely heaquarters for a psychologist, Dr Adrian Atkinson, who claimed to have some unique insights.

In June 2004, 30 people arrived at Edstone Hall to take part in the making of a BBC television series, *Mind of the Millionaire*. The programme would test Dr Atkinson's claim that he could see inside the mind of the millionaire.

Of the 30 people, half were successful millionaire entrepreneurs and half were not. After a series of tests, games and activities, Dr Atkinson was asked to give his assessment. Could he really tell who had the mind of a millionaire and who did not?

Amazingly, without any background information or personal knowledge of these people, he correctly identified 14 of the 15 entrepreneurs. What was he seeing? Why is the mind of an entrepreneur different? What can we learn from being able to look into the mind of the millionaire?

Now, don't get me wrong. This is a book about doing what you love. For some people, that may be enough – you may not want to be a millionaire or to even have moderate wealth. However, you will want be able, at the very least, to make a reasonable living.

It is almost certain that whatever your idea, you will be selling some kind of goods, services or know-how. You will need to become more enterprising. Good things and bad things can be learned from looking into the mind of the millionaire.

Adrian Atkinson speaks in one of those soft, soothing Scots accents, so that if he were a medical doctor you would conclude that he had a good bedside manner. In fact, he is a doctor, although he is a doctor of philosophy – a PhD in Applied Psychology. He was set for a career in engineering and then, at the age of 18, he picked up a book on psychology and had what he describes as an 'aha' moment. He became fascinated by the idea of trying to build models of how and why people behave in the ways that they do. From that moment, engineering ceased to have an appeal.

Over the past 15 years, he has developed and refined the Personal Enterprise Profile (PEP). It is a simple questionnaire that can tell you, with startling accuracy, whether you have the mind of an entrepreneur or not. This idea can make people feel uptight – worried in case they don't have it. This is because we have become conditioned into believing that entrepreneurs are all-conquering heroes and that we should all aspire to being one. As Dr Atkinson points out, it is not nearly as simple as that.

> I think people become millionaires or wealthy in various ways and there isn't just an entrepreneur 'type'. There are entrepreneurs who are one sort and there are enterprisers as well. Then there are people who can create wealth and build wealth by working in an organization; they need the support of the organization. Then there are people that I call technical professionals, who often create or invent a new product or new service. They are not very commercial themselves. I think James Dyson [inventor of the Dyson vacuum cleaner] is one. I don't think he is an entrepreneur; I think he is interested and fascinated by the technicality and the expertise that he has.

The PEP test assigns people to a banding, based upon their characteristics, and the result is shown on a continuum, as in Figure 6.1. This is the profile of a serial entrepreneur, someone who creates one successful enterprise, then another, then another. It is someone who scores well into the 90% zone within the PEP test. But what is it about these people? Are they cleverer than everybody else?

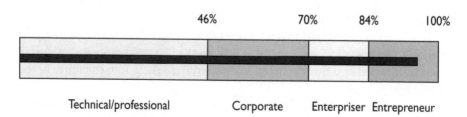

Figure 6.1 *Example PEP test. Reproduced with permission of Human Factors International*

Entrepreneurs are not interested in the technicality or expertise. They are interested in how they can get a commercial result, which I think is a very different thing.

What separates the entrepreneur from the enterpriser is that the entrepreneur is willing to risk everything – even, almost, his own sanity – to achieve what he wants to achieve. The enterpriser will only risk a limited amount: not all of his assets and certainly not his sanity.

So you find enterprisers are people who still go on holiday, whereas entrepreneurs may not go on holiday at all for years and years and years. Even when they are forced to go on holiday by their partners, they tend not to enjoy them, or turn them into work. The danger here, I've always seen, is that when people are talking about entrepreneurs they tend to talk about male entrepreneurs.

According to Atkinson, the female entrepreneur tends to be less obsessive.

Female ones are very, very different.

They don't have this need to risk everything, but they will risk quite a lot – far more than most female enterprisers – but they are not driven by the same thing, they are not motivated by the same things as men are.

Women entrepreneurs are motivated by the need for autonomy and self-development. Those two things are vital to them and they usually have some sort of role model in their past who they can think of – an aunt or a friend who lived nearby, for example – where they thought, 'I like their lifestyle. That's the lifestyle I would like to have.' So they go for that.

The big thing about female entrepreneurs is that they can be contented with life. They can reach contentment. They appear more well-balanced: I guess that some of them aren't, but they are very driven.

I met a female entrepreneur the other day, a very famous one – she started a big IT company in 1962 – and she, at the age of something like 75, is just as driven as she was then. It's amazing how competitive she is. One of the characteristics of being an entrepreneur that male entrepreneurs share is that they are also highly competitive and have a high need for achievement. So they're very ambitious.

It seems that whereas women exhibit entrepreneurial behaviour as part of a process of self-development, men are driven towards entrepreneurial behaviour by some disadvantage or feeling of being excluded, often in their early years. Many entrepreneurs are dyslexic, from poor backgrounds or from minority groups.

The male entrepreneur, the ones that I have worked with – and I have seen research that helps me understand this – strongly suggests that they come from difficult backgrounds. They had some childhood thing that was almost a trauma for them, in a sense, where they suddenly realized, 'Bloody hell, I don't ever want this to happen in my life'. So they go hell-for-leather to create a life that doesn't allow them to go back into that poverty or that 'not being recognized' situation that they felt early on in life – we reckon that 40% of entrepreneurs are dyslexic.

Being dyslexic doesn't make you entrepreneurial, but being dyslexic can give you an experience at school of being marginalized and that's a word that I think is key to entrepreneurs. Something in their childhood marginalized them from the rest of their group.

Creating a successful enterprise and generating wealth are the hallmarks of the entrepreneur, but what is it about a millionaire's mind? Are millionaires actually more intelligent than the rest of the population?

There is a new book that looks at 40 successful entrepreneurs. In the foreword it says that entrepreneurs are far more intelligent than other people. This is absolute rubbish. It is just not true for male entrepreneurs. We've assessed many entrepreneurs and we found that some of them were very, very unintelligent. 'Not very bright' is probably a polite way of saying it.

So you don't have to be highly intelligent, but if you are not very bright, your entrepreneurial flair has to be very focused in an area that you continually work in, because you gain your knowledge and skills by experience. What you find is that the very bright people who are entrepreneurs are able to learn new concepts, new ways of doing things very quickly, so that they can jump from one thing to the other.

One of the key things for the less bright ones is that they should stick to their knitting. If they are making money out of say, the transport business, then don't go into selling insurance, because you won't win.

I have met so many people like this. They don't realize their own limitations. That is a sad thing.

Perhaps this explains why so many entrepreneurs are successful in one field yet go on to lose pots of money in another field.

It's very difficult. I've had entrepreneurs come to me, saying, 'I'm an entrepreneur, I've made money at this, and now I want to go into this. Now how can you help me?' Sometimes I've said, 'Well, the best way I can help you is by telling you, "Don't go into this", because you ain't going to be able to learn quickly enough to make money out of it.' And then they go and do it and lose loads of money. It's a pretty classic thing for people to think that because they have been entrepreneurial in one area, they can make it in any other area.

It's just not true. You have to be very bright. You have to love – be fascinated by – learning new ways of doing things. Duncan Bannatyne, for example, is a very bright guy. He is a very fast learner and is insatiable in trying to learn more. So he tends to be able to move from one thing to another: from ice cream vending, through property, nursing homes, childcare, fitness centres and whatever comes next.

Duncan Bannatyne was one of the entrepreneurs that Atkinson correctly identified for the BBC series. He is described by Atkinson as 'very bright', though he has no formal academic qualifications. He left school at 15 and began delivering bread. Having secured his first mortgage, he bought an ice cream van and used the profits to buy four more houses, refurbishing them as bed and breakfast hostels. He went on to develop a chain of nursing homes that he sold in 1997, netting him £26 million. When he struggled to find a nursery for his children he created a nursery business, making a further £22 million. His current business, Bannatyne Fitness, is estimated to be worth £80 million. Now he says that he is fed up with making money and has trained at RADA and the New York Film Academy because he wants to be an actor. He is reported to have said that one of his motivations is that people don't think he can do it. He wants to prove them wrong.

With stories like this, one would expect these people to be superhuman, yet Atkinson has noticed something.

There are personality characteristics. One of the other misunderstandings about entrepreneurs is that people think they are all self-confident people. Many of them are very self-critical, they are very anxious worriers. They worry things to death and never give up.

In fact, I would say that there are fewer highly self-confident ones. I mean, take Branson for example: he's a shy person. He's got a lot of personal confidence in that he believes he can achieve things, but socially he's actually quite ill at ease.

So it's a very complex question as to what makes an entrepreneur, but there are some basic fundamental things like willingness to take risk. So attitude to risk is an important aspect as to whether you are going to be successful as an entrepreneur or not.

***

The classic entrepreneur, then, is a complex character, often trying to escape from the past, taking massive risks, not always very bright, but with a massive work ethic that could be described as obsessive. Atkinson has spent a lot of time with these kinds of people and is fascinated by them; yet he is the first to admit that, fascinating as they may be, they are not the kind of people that you would want to get stuck in a lift with.

It's their obsessiveness in terms of their egocentrism. They are only interested in achieving what they want to achieve. As long as you show an interest in that and go along with it, you will be a very trusted and liked person. If you start disagreeing with them, saying, 'No, I think you are wrong', they find that very difficult to take. Also, they tend to only talk about what they want to talk about. That's what makes them rather difficult to live with and cope with.

***

Whilst lots of people who run businesses would tend to describe themselves as entrepreneurs, they are in fact what Atkinson has described as enterprisers. These people can create successful businesses, though not on the scale of the entrepreneur, and they tend to take lesser personal risk. However, they are quite often more intelligent than entrepreneurs and work with other people. In short, people who are well-balanced.

Enterprisers need other people to create the wealth and achieve things, so they are people who work with other professionals. They see the value in other people's advice. They are still highly competitive and very driven, but they don't think that life's about achieving their own thing; they see that other people's opinions and advice can be useful in achieving some goal. So they are different to normal corporate people in that they see radical ways ahead. They see radical shifts in how things should work.

These enterprisers are rare. There are maybe 1 in 1000, perhaps even 5000, working in companies. You need them. If you don't have them, the company's going to go down.

There are certain skills associated with being an enterpriser. One of them is being very good at analytic thinking, being able to analyse problems and issues, so that you can see what the assumptions are and you can then work out ways to cover yourself if those assumptions don't hold.

They think, 'In how many ways can this go wrong?'

Atkinson believes that it is very difficult, probably impossible, to learn to become an entrepreneur. You either have those characteristics or you don't. It is possible, though, to move up the scale on the enterpriser zone and in this way develop your millionaire mind.

Critical and analytic thinking skills are an important part of being a very good enterpriser, and that can be taught. Some people have got the personality – they are very bright, they are strategic – but they don't have the speed of analysis to be able to just get there, and we've actually coached people in that particular area.

Other people haven't ever read anything or been trained in strategic thinking, so just helping people to get better at this can make them better enterprisers.

The other thing for them to do is just to realize why they are special, why are they different to other people. What is it that they have got to offer?

Whereas in Chapter 2 we looked at techniques for discovering your passions, it is also useful get feedback from people about what they see as your special characteristics.

Our way of working out why they're special is through our assessments. The other way is to try to find out from other people what they see. How are they seen by other people – what is it that they are good at, rather than just thinking 'I know what I'm good at'? Go and ask your friends, colleagues or your partner. Ask them what is it you're good at, what makes you special, what have you got to offer which is over and above what other people have to offer. We do this in our psychometric assessments. In three-and-a-half hours, we produce a really detailed report.

It is clear from his research on entrepreneurs that their attitude to personal risk is an important defining characteristic. Surely, if people can change their attitude to personal risk, they can get closer to the millionaire mindset. But can people dramatically change their tolerance towards personal risk?

I would say not. What you can do is look at risk and manage risk, and that's what enterprisers and corporate people will do very well. The interesting thing about entrepreneurs is that they don't seem to be interested in managing risk. They just think there's always a way round it, that there's always a solution, and so they always appear to everybody else as very optimistic.

Find out first are you the sort of person who should be doing that [taking risk]? There are different ways to achieve things in life. Maybe you should be trying to invent or create something and sell that to somebody else. Maybe you should be joining a company.

There are different routes. They are not all entrepreneurial and they are not all enterprisers.

It's interesting that for all his work with multimillion pound entrepreneurs, Atkinson draws on an old piece of research to explain how people can be happy and do what they love.

There was an article in 1963 by Gizelli and Georgopolis. For me, it was a very important article, because even psychologists today would say that job satisfaction is the most important thing that you can give your workforce. What I would say from the research is that you can't give people work satisfaction – people get job satisfaction from belonging to a successful team, from being successful themselves. So success creates the job satisfaction. Job satisfaction does not create success.

So you have many people who are very satisfied in their job and are actually very unproductive. You would not by any standard say that they were successful.

They have to go for the thing that they will be able to make the biggest contribution to personal or group success.

I think first they have to have a clear understanding of where they could have success. What should they avoid? What sort of things should they try and achieve? I've recently had a sales guy come to me and said, 'I want to be a manager.' Now this is the normal story you get from everybody, but this is a real guy.

I said, 'If you become a manager you will be a disaster – you just will not be successful and it will make you very unhappy. You have to stick it out and be a better and better salesperson.' That's the key there.

Society provides us with images that we think are the most important ones to go for. It's sexier and higher status to be called a manager than to be called a senior administrator.

It's your personal success that counts. Stick to what you are best at and be highly successful.

Of course, entrepreneurs are lucky, and it is interesting that Atkinson has observed the application of one of Wiseman's four principles of luck at close quarters – turn bad luck into good. In fact, he has seen it applied in its most extreme form.

I think the things that have really stuck in my mind about them is their unwillingness to think that anything is not possible. Now sometimes they are just totally wrong, but they actually believe that they can achieve things. They are not stupid, but if they are going for something, they believe that there is always a way to achieve it, even if a block comes up in front of them. It's that tenacity and resilience that is shown.

Research has shown that the average number of times an entrepreneur starts a business is five. So to be an entrepreneur, you have probably had to fail four times; on the fifth time, you find a successful outlet for your energies and characteristics.

They don't like the word 'fail'. They won't accept 'fail'. I talked to one last week about it and asked, 'How many times did you fail?' He said, 'I've never failed. I've never failed at anything in my life.' It's just a nonsense, because I know him extremely well and he definitely has failed. He's got things going in a way that is just good enough, with £50,000–£100,000 turnover, but it isn't a big business like entrepreneurs want – so that is a failure. Whose definition is it? What they say is. 'It's just not going to go as far as I want, so I'm going to stop doing it.'

But many of them do lose their shirts then start again. I met one in Switzerland. He is a multimillionaire who made £45 million many years ago from scratch cards. He's never succeeded at anything since, and that's from many years ago. When I say 'succeeded', I mean he's not had another £45 million business. He's done a few small things.

Turn the problem into an opportunity. That's what they do. 'We've got a problem, but how can we make this a great opportunity?' That's what they are very resilient at.

Life as an entrepreneur is not all it's cracked up to be – for male entrepreneurs, anyway.

They have a very short-term task focus. They have strategic views in general but are incredibly willing to change their strategies, very willing to change direction.

They get round every problem bit by bit in a very short-term way.

Women entrepreneurs may use mental imagery. They are more likely to think, 'Where will I be in ten years time?' If I'm right about entrepreneurs running away from childhood, then that never stops. They don't have any image of the future: it goes back to the point that entrepreneurs die discontented – they are never contented. They are trying to run away from pain.

Women, though, will head towards a specific situation and once they have achieved it, they feel that they have achieved what they set out to achieve.

If the male feels that they are running away from pain, they don't have the possibility of achieving anything.

So, if Adrian Atkinson is so good at seeing into the millionaire mind, has it done him any good?

There are some people who are theme entrepreneurs; if I was an entrepreneur, I'd be a theme entrepreneur. I'm not interested in businesses that are not related to psychology.

I think that's important in terms of thinking about where you are going to be successful. You still risk everything or anything within that, but what you are doing is applying expertise and knowledge in a particular area fantastically well.

By 1988 we had been going for five years, and I realized that consultancy is really a people business and therefore you had to work to get your money. There was a ceiling in the number of hours you could charge for, so you could never grow except by taking on more and more consultants, and that didn't excite me at all. So I realized that the clever way was to get into the area of assessing people so that you assess people while you are sleeping – anywhere in the world. We needed to have a computerized system to do that, so we were one of the first online assessment companies in the world.

At this moment there are people all over the world filling in our online questionnaire. It gets analyzed; the report gets sent back to them and to the client. It's having that image of how you want the future to be.

What I want to achieve in life is this and the strategy is that. I don't want to be working till I drop.

We test about 5000 people a year from all over the world. It's growing at 40% each year.

The success gives me job satisfaction and if I wasn't successful, I wouldn't be very satisfied at all. It gives me the ability to be interested in the intrinsic motivation of what I do. I don't always have to be in front of a client.

It gives me the time to do the things I want to do.

Adrian Atkinson and his colleagues at Human Factors International continue to search for new and better ways to get into the minds of people and model behaviour. Their tests have proved very accurate and now they are looking at ways to assess people without them knowing that they are being assessed.

Entrepreneurs may not always be bright, but Adrian Atkinson has found a bright way to earn his living doing what he loves – and with his online assessment product, even earns money while he is asleep.

Inside the mind of the millionaire

These insights into entrepreneurial behaviour and attitudes debunk some of the myths that have developed about people who have achieved success using the 'way of the entrepreneur'.

Behind the millionaire lifestyle and the media coverage we see a familiar pattern of male entrepreneurs who are egocentric, obsessive, immensely focused, compelled to continually prove that they are escaping from their early years of being marginalized, practise the science of luck with a vengeance, are driven and, according, to Atkinson 'will die discontented'.

Female entrepreneurs, on the other hand, though highly driven, tend to be driven in a different direction. The male entrepreneur uses his drive to try to distance himself from some injustice or disaffection – something he may never quite achieve. This is an *away* motivation. It is about the avoidance of pain.

The female tends towards a desire to have greater autonomy and self-fulfilment. This is a *towards* motivation. It drives them towards achieving a vision that can be reached and where contentment can be had.

There is something important to be learned from the distinction between male and female entrepreneurs. It is such a simple lesson that it is almost embarrassing to write. It is that old maxim 'money doesn't buy happiness'. We have all heard it hundreds, possibly thousands of times, and it is something that we can all agree with on a conscious level. So often, however – as in the case of male entrepreneurs – our behaviour does not reflect our conscious belief.

I have had people say to me, 'I would rather be unhappy with money, than unhappy without it.' I can understand this sentiment, yet it has a very negative focus. Why not concentrate on being happy?

According to Atkinson, this is really about being clear about what success means to you and achieving it – it need not necessarily be measured in monetary terms. If you can create a *towards* motivation, in the way that female entrepreneurs do, you can become highly focused and feel a sense of success as you progress towards it. If all you ever have is an *away* motivation, don't be surprised if you show the characteristics of many entrepreneurs. That is, as Adrian Atkinson observes, 'self-critical, anxious, worriers who worry things to death'.

So the first thing we can learn from the millionaire mind is that success is more important than money. If we can decide the things that we will count as success and establish positive *towards* motivations, we can enjoy the journey as well as the destination. By getting a well-balanced set of success criteria, it is highly likely that money will follow provided that we concentrate on what's important.

What kind of a mind?

When I first met Adrian, he offered me the chance to undertake the PEP test. I wanted to know if I had the mind of a millionaire. It was interesting. Because I had already heard his explanation of the technical & professional, corporate, enterpriser and entrepreneur typology, I made a guess at where I thought I might be on the continuum. I considered myself to be a strong enterpriser, with a hint of the entrepreneur. The result of my PEP test is shown in Figure 6.2.

It could not have more accurately reflected my own intuitive assessment. You can take the PEP test yourself by going to www.humanfactors.co.uk. Alternatively, you can make your own intuitive assessment by comparing yourself with the broad characteristics of each type.

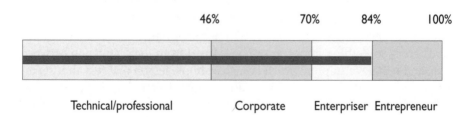

Figure 6.2 *The author's PEP test. Reproduced with permission of Human Factors International*

Technical and professional

These people are highly accomplished in their specialist field. They tend to have an intrinsic fascination with their area of expertise rather than any potential for its commercial exploitation. They are highly risk-averse and tend to be most comfortable in settings where they can focus their energies towards their specialist subject with like-minded people.

Corporate

These people need the strength and security of an organization around them. At the extreme end of this scale are the high-achieving captains of industry who can become extremely successful and wealthy – but they are at their best when they are taking calculated risks with the resources of the organization.

Enterpriser

The enterpriser may work on their own account – running their own business, perhaps – or may be found pushing back the boundaries in corporate organizations. Invariably they are very bright, although not necessarily academically qualified; they are excellent critical thinkers; they can analyze situations quickly and intelligently; and they have the ability to see things strategically.

They are driven by their need for achievement, control, status and dominance, and want fast, significant progress. They want to be top of the league in whatever it is that they do.

They do take some personal risk, but because of their propensity to manage risk, this will not be risk on the scale of the entrepreneur.

They value challenge, independence and being able to demonstrate leadership, and they make fast decisions.

Entrepreneur

These are people who are great to have around as long as you share their view of the world and you don't disagree with them.

They are expedient, often (though not always) socially confident, dominant, experimental, driven, decisive and thrive on risk and challenge. They will take massive personal risk, often in the defiance of any logic, tending to reframe 'failure' and adapt and change their tack to move around any obstacle.

Male entrepreneurs tend to be driven by some experience of being marginalized in their early years, such as being dyslexic or from an immigrant background. Others – often those that were born into poverty – are driven by a sense of social injustice. They are driven by a burning desire never to return to their childhood experiences, their need for autonomy and of course wealth creation.

Female entrepreneurs tend to be brighter overall, with 70% of them being educated to degree level. They seek autonomy and professional self-development. They can achieve a level of satisfaction that male entrepreneurs find difficult to establish.

You are your environment

I watched the BBC series *Mind of the Millionaire* with interest. At the time, I had never met Adrian Atkinson, but as a young man growing up in a pretty tough neighbourhood, I had often thought that a lot of the kids had characteristics that, if they were applied to business, could have made them very successful. Of course, they rarely were.

When I considered the analysis of the millionaires' minds, I became even more convinced of this. Young people in deprived neighbourhoods quite probably have entrepreneurial characteristics. One of my friends, for example, used to specialize in electrical goods. He could get you anything: TVs, videos, spin dryers. The problem was that none of these things actually belonged to him. He did eventually spend some time in prison.

On his release, he told me that it had been a great education. He found himself in an environment with criminals who had much more experience than he had. Their stories, their successes, their failures were all part of the learning process.

Many years later, I had a similar experience myself – not in prison, though! I found myself living in an area awash with enterprisers and entrepreneurs. They all want to talk – especially the entrepreneurs, who only want to talk. What I have noticed is that through a process of listening, analysis, comparison, sorting fact from fiction and experimentation, my attitude to risk, my creativity and my belief has grown significantly. When you are around positive people, their enthusiasm and belief in good fortune seeps in almost like osmosis.

This is very important. If you are going to embark on a life that you can love, it is hard enough, without being surrounded by people who just want to put a negative spin on things.

You are your environment, so you must nurture it. Find people who are similar types to yourself. Surround yourself with people who are doing things similar to what you want to do. Listen, analyze, compare, experiment, adapt.

Create your own learning environment wherever you are – in the pub, the wine bar, your dining room – by bouncing off positive people.

Developing your millionaire mind

Whether you want to become a millionaire is immaterial. It is useful to learn from both the good things and the not-so-good things that go with the millionaire mind.

Try to develop yourself so that you become ever more enterprising by:

- setting clear criteria for success;
- developing *towards* motivations;
- improving your tolerance to risk;
- developing risk-management approaches;
- being tenacious and resourceful when faced with obstacles;
- listen to advice, then be decisive;
- remain flexible and alert to other ways to achieve your objectives; and
- enjoy the journey as much as the arrival at your destination.

When is a millionaire not a millionaire? When he's a social entrepreneur

The work of Adrian Atkinson tells us a lot about wealth creators. He has focused his attention on people who create financial wealth. I believe, though Adrian doubts this, that another kind of entrepreneur exists and is in evidence all over the place if only we choose to notice. These are the social entrepreneurs – people who behave in very similar ways to capitalist entrepreneurs, except their focus is different.

Rather than being focused on wealth creation, social entrepreneurs address their considerable energies and talents towards building 'social capital'. This is the notion of bringing people and their talents together with other assets such as buildings, skills, know-how and money. The purpose? To create a better street, a better estate or a better neighbourhood – a different world.

They don't pursue personal wealth; they are altruistic. Yet as a society, we have become so obsessed with material wealth and possessions that many people have a very hard time just believing that these people actually exist.

Well, we met one in Chapter 4. Andrew Mawson is a man possessed – which is an unfortunate word to use for a clergyman. Yet he has intense focus, high energy, will not entertain the notion of failure, takes risks and definitely passes Adrian Atkinson's 'lift test'. Unless you are passionate about backing people rather than building complex government and organizational structures, you don't want to get stuck in a lift with Andrew Mawson.

To show you that he is not a one-off, and to test Adrian Atkinson's models of enterpriser and entrepreneur in the social context, I'm going to take you to Benchill, a large council estate in Wythenshawe, a suburb of Manchester.

In England, there are deprived neighbourhoods. There are tough neighbourhoods. Then there is Benchill. They don't come much tougher than this place. In 2000, the Government's index of deprivation ranked this estate as top of the league. That's not a great honour to have: it means that it is the poorest, sickest and most run-down neighbourhood in England. The index, though, only tells of measurable social and economic factors. It tells us nothing of what it is like to live there.

One man, a social entrepreneur called Greg Davis, has lived there for most of his life. He has everything that it takes to be a wealth creator and he's proved it. Yet for some reason he is unable to rest. He has that determination, that focus, that irrational optimism of the entrepreneur. And he is driven: not by money, but by a burning desire to make England's worst neighbourhood a better place. To create a glimmer of opportunity. It is what he calls his 'unfinished business'.

Mr January's doing an eight-year stretch

Staring down the barrels of a sawn-off shotgun, Greg Davis, one-time vendor of professional muscle and intimidation, decided that his life – if he was to continue to have one – had to change.

He had established the largest door security agency in the north-west of England. For a young man who had spent his early years in and out of care homes, he had done well. He owned a farmhouse in a select Cheshire suburb, drove a Porsche and a Range Rover, and had an income that others could only dream of.

Now he was a family man. As the drugs scene began to grow, control of the doors meant control of the drugs. This was serious stuff. Greg though was smart; he chose to get out whilst he was still at the top. He had enjoyed little of family life as a child and was determined that his children would grow up knowing their father.

When his first daughter was born, he decided it was time to live a life that he could love. He had no idea what that was. He just set out to find it.

Greg Davis is a remarkable character. Imagine Popeye the sailor man. Now make the image taller. Now make it wider. That's Greg Davis: a formidable hulk of a man who looks as though he has been carved out of granite.

He has, undoubtedly, seen some action in his time, and you get the impression that there are some stories he would rather not tell. Yet he defies the stereotype. When you talk to him, you realize very quickly that this is not some 'iron pumping' jerk high on testosterone. He is a highly intelligent, articulate, softly spoken and clean-living young man who is courteous and respectful.

His conversation is peppered with passages from Shakespeare, references to Karl Marx and biblical quotations. He has turned his entrepreneurial mind towards social goals: towards making the neighbourhood in which he grew up a better place. A place in which amongst the violence, the drug culture, the ill health, the unemployment and the poverty there is a glimmer of hope – a glimmer of opportunity.

Now he proudly sits in what was once a derelict church building. Today it is the home of a project that he calls 'the United Estates of Wythenshawe' (UEW). It houses a gym, a fitness suite, a dance studio, a hairdresser's, a therapy centre and a café; soon it will house a new boxing centre.

It is a high-energy place that pumps out urban rap music. The young men look as if they have been carved from the same piece of rock as Greg. The young women smile politely but give the impression that they too know how to handle themselves. Be in no doubt, this is still a very tough neighbourhood, but the UEW is both a sanctuary from the harsh world that lies beyond its front door and a place to realize opportunity.

All the activities are self-financing and any surpluses fund a food distribution project and support local groups such as the kids' basketball team.

Greg sits by a pile of crumpled UEW calendars. They are crumpled as if they have been used. It seems that they were a fundraising project. Mr Universe-type young men from the gym are pictured in various poses, oiled-up and dressed as policemen, firemen, red Indians and so on, using various bits of gym equipment to protect their modesty.

The calendar? It did extremely well in the Gay Village. Mr November and Mr May, which was me, got quite a lot of fan mail. One bloke in particular. He rang up this year to see if we were doing it again.

We won't be. Mr January going to prison for eight years for armed robbery was one reason, and Mr October was involved in quite a nasty murder – middle of September. The problem we had with that is that every shop's got a calendar up, the hospital's got the calendar up. Come October, the smiling face of a murderer is up in every shop and public place with our logo plastered all over it. We had to withdraw them.

I'm not discouraged. I'm saddened that it's happened, because I know both sets of families. It's a situation that should never have occurred. Somebody lost a life for no reason. It was a stupid skirmish that very quickly boiled over. But we see it happen in this neighbourhood, people get murdered for five or ten pounds. Reputation is so important that they cannot lose ground.

The best way to turn that around, so that the success ladder is there, is by coming to places like this. In here we get complete and absolute respect.

Greg describes his upbringing as 'normal'. Then, on reflection, he considers that he had nothing to compare it with, so it seemed normal. It was far from what most of us would consider normal. Firstly, it was played out between England's toughest neighbourhood and a range of children's homes and hostels. Secondly, few of us have had to have beans on toast on Christmas Day.

Our upbringing wasn't stable. We were brought up in places like Lads' Clubs and then homes a bit later on. It's difficult because I've got no comparison, so I would say it was a fairly normal upbringing.

We were brought up in a naughty boys' home. But that was because there was nowhere else for us to go – it wasn't because we were naughty. But I suspect we were taught quite a lot of naughty tricks by the time we had left there.

Others in Benchill had the same experience, and Greg recalls speaking to one of the local 'hard men'.

I remember being on that bus and I couldn't stop crying. I didn't know if my mum was going to come back for me. Those were our feelings. This character was quite a big name now, yet he had exactly the same feelings as me.

The expectation is that you eat turkey for Christmas and if you are eating beans on toast, you're different from everybody else. It's just not a nice feeling to be separate from everybody else.

On the tape of my interview with Greg, it is clearly discernable that when he reaches the word 'separate', he reserves a special intensity for that word, and elongates it, almost as if trying to pack it with a punch; as if elongating it will give him more time to attack this word.

This feeling of being separate, or feeling excluded at an early age, is something that Adrian Atkinson has noted as a very common feature in entrepreneurs. Greg seems driven not so much to run away from this feeling, but to try to make sure that others don't feel it in the way that he did. That is how the food project emerged.

It's really simplistic. It's an equation. You just have to write it down and put an equals sign at the end of it. Supermarkets will typically throw away a third of their produce in a week. Look at one shelf and think that a third of it is going to be thrown away. It just gets landfilled. So because of my hostel days, and having spent a few Christmases in hostels, it's a very emotive time of the year – sometimes for all the wrong reasons. We brought the two together.

We were given a load of stuff one Christmas. The next Christmas we got mince pies. Next Christmas we got turkeys and potatoes. Then I offered four or five different hostels, including the one I had been at, the chance to have a turkey and mince pies. Each year, it became bigger. This year we distributed 35 tonnes of food – 500 turkeys, 50 tonnes of potatoes, sprouts, everything you could imagine that makes up a Christmas dinner. We gave it away to 51 voluntary groups across the north-west. We fed 2000 people. Nobody pays a penny for this. It's just done through my phone calls.

What developed from this is that supermarkets were coming saying, 'We've got 200 packets of Yorkshire puddings now.' We set up a Fair Share scheme at the back of the building. We've got eight staff in there, all local lads – we tend to target the lads who would struggle with a job interview, would struggle to maintain a typical nine-to-five job.

We are up to eight tonnes of food a week being distributed to those in need from Marks & Spencer, Sainsbury and the Co-op. We pick up every morning from 15 to 20 supermarkets. We have two refrigerated vehicles and comply with all the regulations.

It is charitable work. The income from the gym pays for two part-time van drivers and the others are paid by a grant. We don't even charge an admin fee.

At the very least you would say this is enterprising. The fact that it seems to be driven by Greg's feelings of being different or separated, that he has had to overcome all sorts of barriers and take his opportunities to do it, and that he saw the opportunity, would suggest that it is entrepreneurial behaviour. Yet he doesn't make a penny out of it – nor does he want to. He is a social entrepreneur.

A key part of the make-up of Greg Davis is that he does not become stifled by barriers that may come his way, and he always seems to turn a bad situation into a good one – again, key characteristics of traditional entrepreneurs.

He's always had an eye for the main chance.

By 19, I trained religiously. There was a group of about 25 of us. We did everything but sleep together. A social side built up.

The gym culture grabbed me. Doormen use gyms. It started by people saying to me, 'Could you cover for me for a couple of nights on the door?'

I think it was £30 a night. Twenty years ago, £60 in a weekend was good money for a 19-year-old. Any time there were bits and pieces of work going, I was always the first one to say I'd jump in.

Having got into university, he showed that he was bright, but admits that he felt 'like a fish out of water'. By his second year, he was making so much doing door work that he quit formal education.

It became a business after the third club that I worked at. This was a tough door to work. It could not have been better. It gave you the kind of insight into the trouble that could occur.

It would be fair to say that this was one of the roughest clubs in Manchester. We had different gangs from all the tough areas. There were eight doormen on when normally for a club of this size you would have needed four or five.

People started asking me to bring people in to cover for their nights off. After a while, I realized that I could be making money out of this. This could be a serious business.

I would give the stand-in doormen £5 less than the fee, which I kept. It just snowballed from there. We were the biggest agency in the northwest for seven of out ten years – 140 permanent door staff, probably another 100 on a casual basis.

We were by far the biggest. For two to three years we were a typical small business. What broke us into a larger business was that we had developed a reputation on the inside, amongst the doormen, that we treated our lads well.

Not just giving good wages, which we did. We established the first trade union for door staff.

We had a phone call from an area manger asking how much notice we would need to cover a pub door. 'What about tonight?' he asked. I said we would do it, and I went myself. The first few punters coming in said and things like 'You're brave.' The night before a gang had stabbed the doorman and gave a warning that nobody else should work that door.

Being there the day after made it look as if we were superhuman. We looked as though we couldn't have cared less.

Greg describes what happened next as if it were nothing more than a polite business conversation.

We made the appropriate phone calls, found out who was involved and asked them as politely as possible if they wouldn't do it again, because we were now on the door. If you are from this neighbourhood it does make people think twice about starting any trouble.

Because we had done a good job, the area manager referred us up the line, and without exaggerating we were getting almost a phone call a day asking us to cover a new door. The brewery began getting landlords to contact us. When Boddingtons needed doormen, they phoned us. It was lucrative and glamorous.

A bad situation, a dangerous situation, had been turned into something good – certainly good for Greg's business, which grew and grew. He takes an opportunity and grabs it by the throat – so to speak.

This is exactly what he did when he set off to create a new life for himself. In the centre of Benchill was an old, crumbling church. It had fallen into disrepair and was a target for vandals and 'smackheads'.

This was an empty shell of a building. This was a drug-dealing area. There was no roof on it, it was vandalised to death. A target for kids.

It was a case of do something with it or demolish it. I asked the church to give me the building. They wanted to know what was going to be done. I said that they would just have to trust me and that I'd do something with it. They asked if I could guarantee £8000 a year for the rates assessment. I just said yes, not knowing what I was going to do with the building.

We were giving up a lifestyle. We had a farm in Styal, I drove a Porsche, we had a Range Rover. The lifestyle was fantastic. Yet I was confident that I would do something. I don't think that I was overly worried that things would go pear-shaped.

It sounds like a complete leap of faith. An opportunity was given to us. It made me get out of the door staff business.

So with a derelict building and an uncertain future, what do you do? Where do you start?

The roof was a big issue. You could see the sky through it. If we were going to do anything, we needed to repair the roof. We also needed to guarantee the future of the building. We did the first thing anyone would do – we got quotes ranging from £80,000 to £120,000, and that's going back ten years. If we'd had that money, I wouldn't have wanted to spend it on a roof.

The way we did it was like this. Out of 140 doormen, we had builders, we had roofers, we had plasterers, we had plumbers, we had joiners. I got two qualified roofers. We borrowed a bit of scaffolding, and I won't say who from, because they didn't know it had gone missing – they got it back again a few weeks later. We fixed the roof ourselves.

It cost us £15,000, yet the cheapest quote was £80,000. When we first took the building on I had a vague idea about physical activity use. Later on, we established the idea of it being a public gym and began approaching charitable trusts. We started getting grants, and I find it a big pain in the arse writing grant application forms, but we started to get them.

That seems fine. Yet in the country's toughest neighbourhood, having just repaired the roof of a building, how do you stop it from becoming vandalized again? Greg had learned a lot on the doors. Not just how to handle himself, but how to deal with people, how to spot conflicts and prevent them from escalating, how to be a leader. He knew that he had a big reputation in the area. Not a reputation that everyone liked, but he felt he had the ability to bind people together.

People assumed that I was still doing the doors. The first thing I did was get into contact with the leaders of the area. The leaders at street level are the people on any estate whose houses don't get burgled, whose cars don't get broken into, who have influence, who have persuasive power over the kids. Street leaders. You know who the dominant families are.

There are two types of family. Those that work the doors, and those that fight the doors. We know who they all are. I either knew who they were or we had crossed swords. My first job when I got this building was to contact every kind of problem, nuisance, powerful, persuasive family in the area and get one representative. What's good about that is that they all tend to represent a sport like football, boxing, body-building, powerlifting, judo or wrestling. I'm oversimplifying this. It took quite a long time. My background, experience and reputation helped.

We got them together, and there were one or two people who were not happy about being there, I said, 'Come on, come on.' Some were hostile about meeting with me, and when they found that others were going to be there they just didn't want anything to do with it. We pulled it off eventually. We got everybody who has any kind of name at street level in one room.

It's a bit remarkable. That formed the basis of what you would loosely call the 'management team' for this place.

I told them that the building was mine and the opportunity that you have got is whatever you want to put in this building. I want everybody to be involved.

They bought into it.

Greg once asked me to go to Benchill to give a talk to this management team. I can tell you that without exception, they looked a formidable group of people. They were tough, no doubt, yet they had channelled their energy into producing something for everybody.

We started with a very 'scratchy spit and sawdust' gym. It was a gym that spoke the language, lots of heavyweights. It took off very quickly. It still looked like a church.

Within the first year, we had people joining. I remember the first person joining because it was like someone joining your idea. I should have framed that one really. It was vindication that my idea actually meant something.

The people on the management team would use the place. That was good advertising in itself. It's not long before the kids that aspire to be them – it's cool to be associated – the youngsters began coming in and staying. That worked incredibly well.

It has grown in increments by us living on the estate, knowing exclusively what's missing, speaking to our neighbours, speaking to our customers. Now as well as a state-of-the-art gym, we have a commercial working hairdresser's, we have a fitness suite, therapy rooms, we've just built a dance studio and we've got the café area. It's all run by people who have come in and said, 'You could have a café here and I'd run it', so we built one. And that sounds really simple, and it was as simple as that, because why create barriers when there aren't any?

If somebody comes in and you've got the space, why not try it?

The charity pays me a salary if I do fundraising for that salary. The gym income pays the manager. All the costs are self-contained. We've become a successful centre for local people. The more we can put in this, the less fundraising I have to do.

Another common feature of entrepreneurs is that they can never 'scratch that itch'. It's like that with Greg Davis – he just cannot be satisfied.

What we must do next is roll this out to other communities. The people in an area that are deemed to be the 'baddies': you get them together in a room and squeeze the goodness out of them. What you end up with is a building that all the naughty kids can come and use, and it doesn't get vandalized. What a platform that is if you want to speak to naughty kids. Open the door and speak to them. But we have been totally ignored by the 'authorities'. The people that are in a position to make valuable decisions about this place, have totally, totally disregarded what has been going on.

For Greg Davis, this is just another obstacle in a long line of obstacles that he has had to overcome. He is determined that the model he has developed will be replicated in other tough neighbourhoods. But why, when he had a comfortable lifestyle, does he do this?

As he answers, he leans forward and lowers the tone of his voice so that it is almost a whisper, and takes on an even more deliberate and determined tone.

Because I can. It's because I can. Unfinished business.

We've come a long way … now we've got the vandals on the inside, they actively defend the place. Now what a turnaround. If you can turn the fortunes and reputation of a building around in a place like this, there's not a lot you can't do. In nine years, we haven't had any vandalism.

Definitely. Unfinished business.

Like the male entrepreneurs that Adrian Atkinson has assessed, Greg Davis has that unscratchable itch. His business will never be finished. That is good news for our toughest neighbourhoods.

It confirms my belief that the mind of the entrepreneur is not just the mind of the millionaire or in pursuit of wealth. The mindset is very similar to the mind of the social entrepreneur: developing social capital by joining things together and making something out of nothing.

Staring down the barrels of a sawn-off shotgun, as Greg Davis did, is a bad situation. He has turned bad luck into good, just as entrepreneurs have a knack of doing. He has also created a life that he loves.

7

Think like an eight-year-old

Robert Swan stood on the South Pole. He had achieved a dream that he had carried with him since he was a boy. He had lived into his job description, which says simply 'adventurer'.

Surveying the scene, he grasped two handfuls of ice. He clenched it in his hands. It began to melt. The icy water trickled through his fingers.

Then it was gone.

'Life,' he thought, 'is like that. It can trickle through your fingers, and before you know it, it is gone.'

What better reason to follow your dreams? What better inspiration than an adventurer who has been prepared to overcome all kinds of obstacles to do what he loves? And what better way to do it than to rediscover the magic, the creativity, the possibility that we have when we are children?

Can you remember what you were doing when you were eight years old? Being eight years old is a very special time. You are old enough to imagine and still naïve enough to believe that anything is possible.

This is a beautiful naivety. It is a time when our imaginative powers are at their height. It is a time when we have a belief beyond reason. A time before we become constrained by our teachers, our parents, the expectations of our peers, the need to pass exams, the implication that there is *one* right answer and the pressure to conform and 'do well'.

Before we know it, we have been tested, compared, constrained and then locked into an 'adult' mindset. Often, this leads us to becoming trapped in a life that we hate and that we cannot think our way out of.

How can we rediscover the heightened imagination and belief beyond reason of the eight-year-old?

Far from being just a fanciful idea, this is a very important question. People who are successful tend to think highly creatively and also develop an unshakeable belief. Often others see this as akin to the naïve belief of the eight-year-old.

To do what you love and earn money from it, you will have to continually enhance your ability to think creatively and develop an unshakeable belief, when all around you think you are crazy.

Robert Swan's dream took root in his early childhood – and if ever there was an example of unshakeable belief, this is it. In 1986 he walked in the footsteps of Captain Scott to the South Pole because he watched the film *Scott of the Antarctic* when he was a child. Entranced by the film, he instantly decided that is what he would be – an adventurer. He later became the first man in history to walk to *both* poles. His dream now is to make his contribution to the last great exploration on earth – how to survive on it. He intends to save Antarctica.

He is a whirlwind of a man. He speaks deliberately and loudly, in the style of a headmaster bellowing across the playground. He has an obsession with his passion, which is hugely infectious. And it all began, one afternoon, when an imaginative child settled down on the sofa and John Mills appeared on the screen.

I saw a film called *Scott of the Antarctic* starring John Mills, the famous British actor, and when I watched that film it fascinated me about these bloody people. It was like, what the hell … it was like I sat back and I thought, Wow! Now this is something. This is extraordinary. What the hell are these people doing in Antarctica? And I started to look at the map and thought, Wow! This is really out there. This is something that is amazing. It really captured my imagination. Not only the place – but these people. A bit like, without being silly, when people hear I'm coming to do a talk they think, what the bloody hell's this guy on? They think it's interesting, or really odd, or completely f****** stupid.

It created for me that sense of Wow! The Wow! factor. This is a really amazing feeling inside. The place, that all I'd ever seen was on the map, a sort of white finger sticking out from the bottom of the world. Here was a story that was off the map.

That absolutely captured my imagination and there was an element of a physical challenge. I was always a very physical chap and there was that sense of seeing Captain Scott's teeth and the chin, and the 'Come on chaps, we can do it.' There was a bit of that involved.

Not from an egotistical point of view or a British Empire bollocks point of view – it was just here was a fantastically physical challenge. That interested me.

Most of us as children have seen a film and been inspired. We may have even gone outside and acted out the roles. Robert Swan was so taken by the whole thing that he decided that he would be just like the men on TV.

Luckily, he found himself in a space and a place where he didn't have his dream knocked out of him.

> I was lucky. I went to a public school. Not a big fancy one, but a public school where that sort of thing wasn't too much out there. It was still old-fashioned in many ways. It was called Sedburgh School. Will Carling, the famous rugby player, went there. It was a tough place.
>
> It had a sort of feeling about it that it was possible to say that you were going to be a polar explorer. Because it was old-fashioned and had values and it was a great school. People didn't go, 'Oh well, you must be f****** mad'; it was, 'Well, how are you going to plan for it? Do you know what you are taking on there?' It was a piece of luck.
>
> I was lucky with my family too. I'm number seven in the family. As we all know, number one is a shitty place to be in the family, because everybody panics – when you get to number seven, as I was, you could have said 'I'm going to implode on the road', or 'I'm going to make water into wine', or 'I'm going to make gold out of rocks', and people would just say 'Yer, alright mate. Carry on.' Because you're number seven.

So, he was able to carry on with this belief that he was to be an adventurer. Later in life he found this made him amazingly popular with girls at parties: a double incentive to make it happen. However, you can't just finish your education and pop down to the Job Centre to see if there are any vacancies for adventurers: he had to shape his own destiny.

> We raised £3 million. One has to have this ability to make money or keep your head above water. If you haven't got a silver spoon in your mouth, then to live your dream you almost have to have something that keeps you going while you get the dream.
>
> One lives and learns, and I tried for several years to raise money from companies and eventually I had to research all the companies – this was the big breakthrough, this was if you like the magic break – it was when I suddenly thought, 'Hang about, Captain Scott must have had sponsors, so let's research who sponsored him and go back nearly a hundred years later and find out if they would like to sponsor us.' Now that took a hell of a lot of research, because people like Scott didn't have sponsors lists.
>
> So I researched who'd sponsored him and managed to start the ball

rolling, getting companies to sponsor me in celebration of what they had done for Scott.

People like Colman's of Norwich. All the old companies: Cadbury's and Barclays Bank were involved, as was Shell. A lot of them didn't know they had supported Scott so I had to remind them.

It was all done to follow in the footsteps of Scott and get to the South Pole, there was no other reason at all. It was a very practical mission.

There was no issue, except to do it. That was enough for the first dream. What you've got to do to live your dream, you've got to be able to adapt the dream, and like any business meet the marketplace for dreams.

At the age of 28 he finally set out with a small expedition onboard their boat, *Southern Quest*, a former whale catcher, to conquer the South Pole.

They trekked more than 1200 kilometres in 70 days to get to the pole, pulling sledges twice the weight of an average man. They consumed 5100 calories a day and still lost weight on the way to the pole.

They had been prepared for crevasses, frostbite and temperatures down to –70°C. What happened to them, though, came as a massive shock. Swan's eyes changed colour as he walked to the South Pole under a hole in the ozone. The light reflecting up off the snow burned his eyes and caused them damage. His face was, as he puts it, 'fried off'. They were astounded by how much debris, toxic waste and rubbish had been abandoned there.

They finally reached the Amundsen–Scott base at the South Pole, where they heard that their supply ship, *Southern Quest*, had been crushed by the ice pack in the Beaufort Sea and had sunk.

They had to be airlifted off the pole, picking up the crew of *Southern Quest* on the way. Swan had been appalled by the way Antarctica had been used as a dumping ground, and in 1987 raised more money so that he could go back in order to remove all traces of the base he had left behind. The aircraft, the base hut, stores and rubbish were all shipped out.

He had realized his childhood dream. He had also realized that you have to continually create new dreams.

Walking to the South Pole was a great dream for me then. I had to then adapt it and start to think of other issues such as the environment, or young people – I had to bring in those elements.

So the first expedition was very traditional: get out there, crack on. The second one was again to be the first to walk to both poles. That was the marketing thing, but this time it would have an environmental element, it would have a young people's element.

That's a very important thing. You can say we started off with a very simple thing. Reached the South Pole – bit of history, very British. But that probably wouldn't have carried us on much further. So what we had to do was develop the story. Firstly, to become an international expedition and go to the North Pole. Three Brits went to the South Pole; eight people from seven nations went to the North Pole. That was adapting: we had young people at the base camp, looking at issues that mattered to people, and adapting the story to fit.

He will always be in the history books as the first man to trek to both poles. In 1987, he was awarded the Polar Medal by the Queen, and he received an OBE in 1995.

He had to fight another big battle, though. The man who trekked his way into history struggled to handle everyday life on his return home. His colleagues who described him as 'in his element' during the trek noticed some alarming changes in his behaviour back home. He began to drink heavily and shut out friends, showing the classic symptoms of depression in high achievers.

His dark days cost him his marriage, but he soon regained his sense of focus. He founded Mission Antarctica, a charity set up to inspire environmental action around the world. In 1996 he led 35 young people from 25 nations on an Antarctic expedition to remove 1000 tonnes of rubbish from Bellingshausen Beach on King George Island. Many expeditions later, the project continues to work on removing a major environmental threat.

He had the naïvety of an eight-year-old. He had an unshakeable belief and took a creative view of any problem he faced.

So how can we rediscover our natural creativity? How can we undo those mental locks that are constraining what we think about and how we think?

How can we build a belief beyond reason that will take us towards earning our living by doing what we love?

Roger Von Oech is an expert on creative thinking. In his book *A Whack on the Side of the Head: How You Can Be More Creative*, he weaves a story whereby a teacher and a student are discussing a problem. Despite a lengthy conversation, the student doesn't seem to grasp the point that the teacher is trying to make. Finally, the teacher picks up a stick and gives him a whack on the side of the head with it. Suddenly, the student begins to grasp the situation and 'think something different'.

According to Von Oech, for some of us, sometimes, nothing short of a whack on the side of the head can dislodge the assumptions that keep us thinking 'more of the same'.

How often this is true. How often we wait for something painful to happen – a divorce, a death in the family, being made redundant – before we actually decide to think differently. In fact, when you read through the case studies in this book, it is a common theme. They describe being 'burned out', at their lowest ebb or unhappy. These emotional 'whacks' are at least as painful as the whack of the stick described by Von Oech.

Yet why wait for something bad to happen before thinking more creatively? When we do this, we are trying to be creative whilst experiencing pain or fear – or both. We can, if we want to, find ways to think like an eight-year-old that are pleasurable.

For those who earn their living by doing what they love, thinking like an eight-year-old comes in useful all the time. For example:

- when we are trying to work out what we want to do with our lives;
- when we hit a particular problem or obstacle;
- when we are developing new products and ideas;
- when we are developing sales strategies;
- when we are feeling down or discouraged; or
- when we are feeling successful and want to lift our lives to the next level.

After many years of practising the art of thinking like an eight-year-old, I realized that I had graduated in 2004. I was having a conversation about this and that with my eight-year-old son Callum. Unexpectedly, he stopped the conversation. He looked at me, almost as if he was a little concerned, and said, quite calmly, 'Dad. You're like a child.' At first, I felt a little affronted. Then I realized something. For an eight-year-old to see you as an eight-year-old is the highest praise you can get when you earn your living mostly by thinking about things.

This was high praise indeed. It had happened after years of experimenting; believing that there is always a way; ignoring cynics (and these people are all around us); doing some illogical, crazy things; and in the process learning that life and love can come together. Just as long as you learn to think like an eight-year-old.

To help you towards the day when you can earn your living by doing what you love, you can develop and enhance a whole range of attitudes, behaviours and beliefs in order to think like an eight-year-old. Don't expect it to happen in an afternoon – although it might. Just try things whenever you get the chance.

The more you practise, the more success you will have. The more success you have, the more you will be encouraged to think like an eight-year-old.

Enjoy the process of rediscovering that wondrous, imaginative, naïve, creative and indefatigable child that you once were. Celebrate the small successes that come along the way. Above all believe. So, here are eight ways to help you rediscover your creativity. They sometimes work one by one, often you might combine several methods – what you choose to do depends upon the situation and what works best for you. Treat it as a list of ingredients which you can mix and match according to the way you feel.

One: Fight for the right to be wrong

Teachers: they have the power to inspire. They also have the power to imprison: to imprison us in the chains of 'adult' thinking. Let's not be too hard on them; they are only doing the job that they are being asked to do, and their lives and their latitude to inspire are being eroded all the time. As Government attempts to produce more uniformity and overall 'better' standards, more testing and more targets have become embedded into the culture of education.

There is a growing emphasis on conformity. Children are assessed and compared earlier and earlier. We are nurtured to find *the* right answer to the point that we can feel uncomfortable if we think something which is different from what everybody else is thinking.

When we are trying to be creative we have to reverse this idea that there is a single right answer by telling ourselves that there are many right answers.

Some years ago, I began running 'Creativity Clinics', one-day workshops for public-sector managers – people hardly renowned for being at the cutting edge of new thinking.

To start, I held up an empty tomato soup can, and asked the participants 'What could this be used for?' The response was pretty consistent time after time. There was a long, uncomfortable silence, often interrupted when somebody said something like, 'To put soup in.' Which of course is 'the right answer'.

When you do the same with a bunch of eight-year-olds, they don't hold back. Neither do they look for the obvious. In fact it will probably be the 28th or 35th call before someone says, 'To put soup in.'

They derive positive joy from finding all the alternative uses for this soup tin: a pencil holder; a flower vase; a stilt for a one-legged person; a toilet; a drum; a rolling pin; a biscuit cutter; one half of a string telephone; a cup for rinsing your hair; a stool; and so it goes on. In a very short time, you have racked up dozens of ideas without any effort.

Interestingly, after the awkward silences and the reluctant right answer, public-sector professionals slowly begin to accept that it is OK to have an answer that is not the established 'right answer'. They then begin to get into the swing of things. The pace begins to quicken, and even people who work in bureaucracies begin to remember how to think creatively. Importantly, they begin to realize that they can have fun too.

This can be another area of difficulty. Often people feel that if they are having fun then they cannot be working. This causes them to feel uncomfortable, guilty, self-conscious and as if they are idlers.

We have to reverse this proposition. When work stops being fun, it really is time to stop doing it. If you are struggling with this idea, it is something to work on, because it is an essential proposition of this book, and an essential element of a life that you can love.

If you want to, you can now do two things. First, get your creative juices flowing and begin to think like an eight-year-old. Then note down the many right answers to the observation 'Why work can be fun'. See how many 'right' answers you can find. Enjoy the process. It is not a test, you cannot be wrong.

If you are sceptical about the idea that work can be fun, this is your chance to develop a new vision of work. On the other hand, if you are excited by combining fun with work, this is a chance to create an even more compelling vision of a life that you can love.

Either way, you will begin to get your creative juices flowing. You are on your way to being able to bring back your eight-year-old self.

Two: To create you have to destroy – don't get trapped by the 'rules'

When the National Health Service (NHS) was created in 1948, a disparate arrangement of services, professionals and facilities was brought together under a single structure.

In those days, there was a strong demarcation of knowledge between specialist consultants, general practitioners (GPs) and nurses; information was paper-based and contained in bulky documents; access to information and the flow of communication was very slow.

A system was established. Patients would see their GP and if it was thought that they might need a hospital admission, they would be sent for an outpatients appointment. The consultant specialist would look at them and, if an admission was required, they would be put on the waiting list. During their stay in hospital, they would be looked after by nurses.

More than 50 years on, the world has changed. Clinical protocols and decision-making aids have blurred the boundaries of knowledge so that some consultant knowledge can be GP knowledge and GP knowledge can be nursing knowledge. Information is now less likely to be in a bulky document in the remote cellar of an out-of-the-way hospital. More likely, it can be moved around electronically in an instant and professionals can communicate in real time.

Despite these massive advances in knowledge-sharing and communication, until very recently it was almost as if the NHS was suspended in a 1948 time warp. The rules for out-patient engagement were the same.

Then some enterprising doctors in the Midlands challenged the rules. With access to a clinical protocol agreed with the consultants, GPs could decide which patients were suitable for admission to hospital and put them directly onto the waiting list. Such a simple idea, it makes you wonder why no-one had thought of it before.

This saved the patient an anxious wait for an out-patient appointment and a journey to the hospital, and got them onto the in-patient waiting list months earlier. For the consultant, it saved the time of many hundreds of out-patient appointments every year.

It happened because somebody questioned long-standing, established rules and decided to break the pattern. Yet, despite the efforts of these innovators, for the most part the established way of doing things is still the norm for most of the NHS.

The trouble is, we get comfortable with established rules and procedures to the point where we cannot see any other way.

It's a good idea to challenge your own patterns and rules. Begin to note some of them. Then run the rule over your rules and patterns. For example:

- When I began my new way of life, I set up an office and kept to office hours – because that is what I had always done. Then I realized I could challenge that rule. If I was to do great things with great people and to live on ideas, it could take place anywhere and at any time. I could work when it was raining and play when the sun was shining. I could have an idea in the pub or the post office. I even once had an idea for a successful conference in a dream – I typed it into my PC in my pyjamas at 5 a.m.

- 'You can't wear those clothes, they're your best' was a rule that my mother established. Only in recent years has it dawned on me that I can break this rule. Why postpone happiness? Now each time I travel to London I buy several hand-made shirts from Jermyn Street – and I wear them.

- 'You've got to put in the hours to be successful' was one of my beliefs. I changed this to 'You have to do the right things to be successful.' Sometimes this involves a massive effort; sometimes you can do it in a blink.

Take a look at your familiar beliefs and patterns and consider the following points for each:

- How can I challenge this rule/pattern?
- Decide which rules you want to discard – get rid of anything unhelpful, draining or limiting

Do remember that challenging the rules has its dangers. Some rules may be unhelpful, but they help to keep in place something that you value. You may have to compromise. Only you can decide.

Three: Laugh and the whole world laughs with you

Having fun with ideas can make you laugh. It can also open your mind to new thoughts about how to solve that uncrackable problem or how to get alongside that elusive client. Yet so often we feel that it is wrong to have fun while we are at work.

Film-maker David Puttnam is quoted as saying:

The most exciting creative period of my life was in the early 1960s at the Collett Dickinson Pearce advertising agency when I was group head, working with Charles Saatchi, Alan Parker and Ridley Scott ... But the only thing I remember doing a lot of was tap dancing. We spent hours practising tap dancing and in between we'd work out an ad ... We'd be screaming with laughter, absolutely falling about and meanwhile creating some very remarkable work.

Humour serves a number of purposes. It stretches our thinking, it forces us to combine ideas that are not normally related and it just allows us to take things less seriously.

Maybe we can't all tap dance at work, but we certainly can make our workplaces fun to be in and we can play with our problems.

Some years ago, I was a partner in an up-and-coming management consultancy. The usual process for winning work was to prepare a proposal, which could take two weeks worth of effort, and then, if we were shortlisted, make a presentation to the client. The effort and costs of just competing in the business were huge. After a fifth consecutive second place in such competitions, the mood amongst the partners was dismal.

A meeting was called and the mood was bleak. How were we going to break this cycle of coming second?

Some of the staff suggested re-branding – perhaps a new logo would help. The partners' despondency deepened as they mentally calculated the costs of re-branding.

Then someone began to play with the problem. 'I don't know if you saw the football last night, but every time Lineker got into the danger area, he scored'. Another joined in. 'Yes, but look at our recent track record: every time we get into the penalty box, we seem to whack the ball over the bar. We keep falling down at the presentation stage.'

This caused a laugh and then others joined in. 'Our approach play is excellent, and we've got fantastic people who are able to get the ball in the box. The England manager would go berserk if his strikers missed as many opportunities as we did.' The mood was lightening quickly now. 'Yes, he would have all the strikers in with a specialist coach, concentrating on shooting practice.'

Then Mr Sensible tried to get control of the fun mood that was enveloping the room. 'That's all very well, but that's football. You remember we came here to discuss our performance in presentation, and presentations are –' Before he could dampen the spirits, another voice grabbed his sentence and pulled it back into the fun zone: '… Presentations are like acting. So why don't we learn to act?' Everybody laughed at the idea of developing thespian tendencies, yet before the laughter had died an actor was found and the whole company attended a two-day workshop.

That laughter and fun was responsible for the company becoming a force within its sector. It developed a particular reputation for lively, engaging and imaginative presentations.

It was all because somebody played with a problem.

Four: Fools rush in

Something that holds so many people back is the fear of looking foolish. We can learn from fools though, and we can become more creative if we are prepared to look foolish occasionally.

Conformity causes us to go along with the crowd. It is common for people to adopt 'groupthink' – that condition where we are more concerned with fitting in with the group than we are with coming up with a new idea.

One of the ways to avoid this condition is to 'reverse the proposition'. Whatever you are thinking about, find a way to reverse your viewpoint.

For example, when a group of design consultants sat down with their client to think about the next generation of power drills, it started quite predictably. They looked at size, shape, weight, how to make them more female-friendly. Then someone stood up, drilled a hole in a piece of wood and peered through the hole he had made. He asked the question 'Are we in the business of selling drills or selling holes? Because if we are in the business of selling holes, this technology was around in Jesus's time.'

In reversing the proposition, he risked looking foolish, but he forced the group down another track of thinking. How else could they sell holes – domestic-scale laser beams, perhaps?

Being foolish may not give you the answer you need or solve your problem, but it will get you out of your rut of thinking the same old thing.

Occasionally, be a fool and see what crazy ideas you come up with.

Five: Switch off your logic button

Grown-ups tend to like logic. It helps us to make sense of things, extrapolate and plan. It does not help us to be creative.

Traditionally, logic is based upon the law of non-contradiction. It helps in our understanding of things that are consistent and non-contradictory in their nature. Have you noticed how children love to look for and point out contradictions?

The thing is, most things in life are in fact ambiguous. The number of things that can be thought about in logical terms is relatively small, yet as adults we have a tendency to try to apply logic wherever we can and we inhibit our thinking.

If we want to be creative, we have to learn to switch off our logic button. This is important because great ideas tend to happen in two distinct stages. First, the 'imaginative phase', which is about thinking something different. This is about soft thinking often using metaphor. It is the world of the eight-year-old, where anything is possible, and nobody is going to punish us for thinking outlandishly.

When we have some ideas that we think are worth taking further, we can move into the 'practical phase'. This is about using hard thinking to assess the feasibility of the idea, how it could be implemented, what tasks would have to be set in train to see it through to fruition. It is about getting things done.

In my Creativity Clinics, people can at first feel very uncomfortable in the imaginative phase. Their natural instinct is to get out of it. They want to 'get down to brass tacks', they yearn to be sensible, yet without an imaginative phase they will never break new ground.

Some people will make a token gesture to being in the imaginative phase and then will jump out of it too soon.

In the run up to the Millennium, this happened in a most public fashion. The British Government decided to commemorate this historic event by building a huge dome. A site was selected from a shortlist and construction began at Greenwich in London. Other than being a bold statement for a bold new era, nobody had quite decided what exactly would happen in London's Millennium Dome.

Teams of creatives, thinkers, celebrities and academics were brought together to give life to the inside of the Dome.

There were very mixed opinions about the quality of the Millennium Dome experience. Whilst some visitors were impressed, others described it as shambolic and even downright dull. The visitor attendance figures tell the real story. These failed to reach the wild expectations for this showpiece. As well as costing £800 million to build, the Dome attracted just 4.5 million visitors compared with the predicted 12.5 million, and ended up losing £900 million of taxpayers' money.

This was a classic case of somebody coming up with a germ of an idea and then jumping from imaginative phase to practical phase too soon. Somebody wanted to 'get down to brass tacks'.

Despite all the political goodwill behind it, the power of the best financial and creative brains available, nothing could prevent the Dome from becoming an unmitigated, perhaps unprecedented, disaster.

Maybe if they had just stayed comfortable in the imaginative phase for a little longer, something amazing could have been created. Instead, they got practical and began to build.

The results can be seen in Greenwich today. A crumbling skeleton of the £800 million Millennium Dome lies rotting. Nobody wants to buy it and it is costing Britain's taxpayers millions of pounds a year just to maintain it.

One of the amazing things about political projects that go wrong is that nobody seems to carry the can. Millions of pounds were paid to advisors and yet nobody seems to be asked to pay the money back. History shows that they got it wrong.

The difference with your ideas, when you earn your living by doing what you love, is that you, and only you, are responsible for success or failure.

Learn to get comfortable staying in the imaginative phase: it really is a delightful place to be. Once you have a set of ideas that are rich in detail, that excite you – because if they don't excite you, why should they excite anybody else? – that intuitively feel right to you, then, and only then, move them into practical phase and prepare to take action.

To condition yourself into being more and more comfortable in the imaginative phase, develop some metaphors about anything you want – your work now as compared with your work in the future; you as a person; your family; life; your local restaurant or bar; and 47 other things.

Getting into the imaginative phase is a bit like learning to meditate. At first, people find it hard to get into a meditative state: they become distracted and return to the reality that they know. After some conditioning, people can enter a meditative state rapidly and with ease. They also tend to stay there for longer.

When you learn to be comfortable in the imaginative phase, the word 'bored' will not be needed anymore. Traffic jams, long train journeys and even the dentist's waiting room can be places where you move your ideas around like an eight-year-old would rearrange their toys, creating new scenarios, adding bits, taking away, including things that defy logic or reality, and having a great time.

Six: Be an explorer

It's amazing how many people in the Creativity Clinics stick up their hands when asked the question 'Are you a specialist?' Probably as many as 70% of people who work in the public sector are specialists of one kind or another – doctors, scientists, dentists, nurses, planners, architects, surveyors and many others.

The whole world is becoming more and more specialized. It's how we cope with complexity. The difficulty, if we want to be creative, is that as specialists we develop very specialized behaviours. We mix with the same kinds of people, we deal with the same kind of clients and we focus on the same kinds of issues.

This narrowing of focus often prevents people from looking in other areas. It is limiting.

To feed our creative machine we need to develop an explorer's attitude; we need to look for ideas from elsewhere that can crossover into our sphere. This is often how novel solutions to old problems materialize.

Notice what happens when you are trying to clear out the garage with an eight-year-old. You are trying to load all your junk into the back of the car; they are pulling things out of boxes, trying on hats, asking what a gramophone record does. Eventually you get to the tip. You want to achieve your objective: ditch the junk and get back to pick up the next load. The eight-year-old, meanwhile, finds a snakebelt, peers into an old washing machine and finds some television valves and imagines they are aliens. You are in a hurry, you are focused and you have things to do.

Slow down.

How often are we like this in life – too busy trying to achieve our objective to notice all the unusual, interesting, quirky things around us? Things that, if we thought about them in a different way, might help us to find some novel insights that would take our thinking down a different track.

Try to meet people from different walks of life with different insights and look for the crossover. Over the years, as I have developed my own ideas on leadership and management, I have found useful insights by meeting with the conductor of an orchestra, a polar explorer, a karate champion, a psychologist, a footballer, a politician and many others – all of whom you would expect would have little to contribute other than in their specialist field.

Read things outside your usual sphere, look at the wanted ads, go somewhere that you have never been to before, try listening to a different radio station, talk to a different generation, visit a scrapyard, invite people to lunch or dinner from other walks of life and just ask them to do nothing more than talk. Not only will you feed your creative imagination, you will also make a lot of new friends – people love to talk about what they do to someone who listens attentively.

Whatever you do, store away those little insights and experiences. They might not add up to much right now, but one day you will combine this idea with that, one insight with another, and – eureka! – your explorer's attitude will be helping you to earn your living by doing what you love.

Seven: Take some risks

Since 1994, the National Lottery has distributed £14 billion to projects that are considered to be good causes. This money is not given away lightly. Each applicant completes an application document and has to specify a range of output and outcome measures so that the success of the project can be monitored and assessed.

Since then, the National Lottery has supported more than 50,000 projects. Many of these are new projects that are untried and untested – and therefore risky. One would expect with this volume of projects that some would fail. It would seem only natural.

Yet, according to the Department of Culture, Media and Sport, very few projects ever report that they have failed. How can this be? Does the National Lottery have a magic formula that always turns risk into success? Of course not.

Some people get creative in the way that they interpret and report the outputs and outcomes. Why? We live in a culture where failure is a bad thing. Nobody wants to be seen to fail.

It stems from the 'right answer' culture that we pick up in school. We are conditioned to bury our errors and not talk about them. We hope that they will melt away and not stick to us.

Benjamin Zander, the conductor of the Boston Philharmonic Orchestra, encourages his students to be open about their mistakes. They are asked to try new things; if they don't work out, the students shout 'How fascinating, I made a mistake.' To the creative thinker, a mistake is fascinating: it may lead them to a new way of thinking about something or be a stepping stone to a new idea.

Of course, there are places where errors are inappropriate. We don't want the surgeon to experiment and make mistakes whilst we are lying on the operating table. The creative process is a place where errors are welcome – how fascinating!

Eight: Believe you are creative – and you will be

Roger von Oech relates the story of an oil company that was concerned about the lack of creative productivity amongst its engineers. A team of psychologists was drafted in to find out why some engineers were creative and others were not.

Over a period of three months, the engineers were assessed, analyzed and interviewed. Researchers looked at everything from their educational background to their favourite colours. Their findings were simple and startling. There was one main factor that separated the creative people from the rest:

> The creative people thought they were creative, and the less creative people didn't think they were.

This is very similar to one of the principles of luck. The less creative people didn't believe that they could be creative, so they rarely put themselves in the situation where they could be. They created a self-fulfilling prophesy.

In the language of luck, the creative people created more 'chance opportunities': there were, then, more chances that some of their creative ideas would work. They thus reinforced their belief that they were creative. They created a different kind of self-fulfilling prophesy.

Now we are eight

We were all eight years old once. We know instinctively how to think creatively. We can rediscover that joy, that possibility, that richness of thought that can lead us into fantastic new areas of opportunity.

If we are to earn our living by doing what we love, we must cultivate, every day, our abilities to think like an eight-year-old.

We can, if we fight for the right to be wrong; don't get trapped by the rules; laugh at our problems; prepare to look foolish; switch off the logic button; be an explorer; take some risks; and create a self-fulfilling prophesy – that we are creative.

You will be amazed at what happens when you rediscover that marvellous, naïve, indefatigable eight-year-old that you once were – and still are.

8

Does van Nistelrooy slouch?
Learn to get yourself into the zone

On April 16, 2003, London's Highbury Stadium was the venue for a fixture in English football's Premiership. On the face of it, it was a normal fixture in a season that encompasses 38 matches for each team in the division.

That is, if there could be such a thing as an ordinary fixture between the two teams involved. Arsenal had established themselves as London's top team, and were the reigning Premiership champions. Their opponents were Manchester United. They had become bitter rivals.

United came to Highbury knowing that defeat would tip the scales in Arsenal's favour and they would suffer the indignity of watching their London rivals hold onto the Premiership title. Anything other than defeat would put United in the driving seat.

In the player's tunnel, there is one man who waits expectantly for the game to start. He is Ruud van Nistelrooy, United's Dutch striker. He has a sense that this will be his night; that his moment will come.

After the game, in an interview with Andrew Longmore for *The Sunday Times*, van Nistelrooy talked about the build-up to the game. The night before, he had found himself in his hotel room, playing it over and over in his mind. 'I was in my hotel room watching television, and suddenly I was just there, thinking about the situations that might happen,' he said. 'What to do when I received the ball; playing against Martin [Keown] and Sol [Campbell], thinking about that; I was already with the game.'

Van Nistelrooy's moment arrived after 24 minutes. It was just as he had imagined it: a turn of the right shoulder, a flick and he was clear. 'That was the moment I felt in control. Sometimes, if you are not so confident, you stop. But I just went quicker.' He scores. It is 1–0.

Arsenal equalized with a freakish first goal and then, to United's horror, the referee allowed a player to score a second goal from an offside, illegal, position. It looked like being a night of despair for Manchester and a night of elation for London.

Then United's Ryan Giggs pulled a goal back: it was 2–2. If you watch the video of that game, you will see Giggs reel away in celebration. Unusually, a United player fishes the ball out of the Arsenal goal and returns it to the centre spot. He wants to get on with the game. He wants it to restart.

It is van Nistelrooy.

That night, van Nistelrooy was at the height of his powers. He was, as sportspeople often say, 'in the zone', operating in a heightened state of physical, mental and often spiritual well-being.

The goal gave United a very important point, which turned the tide of the Premiership title race. One month later, Manchester United were once again the Premiership champions.

What is this heightened state called 'the zone'? How can we, whatever we do in life, consistently get ourselves into the zone, where we perform at a heightened level and feel great about it? How can we use our ability to get into the zone to help us live a life that we can love?

Many of us have had incidents in our lives quite the opposite to the situation described by Ruud van Nistelrooy. Instead of feeling in control, we have felt powerless. He points out that when you are not so confident, you stop: this happens not just in football but in life. When we are not so confident, we stop chasing our goals, we lose belief. We dither. We don't achieve.

Athletes, florists, chefs, accountants, lawyers, artists, doctors, tradesmen, writers – in fact, anyone – can achieve fantastic things when they are in the zone. When they are not in the zone, they can experience fear, anxiety, lack of belief and frustration. All negative things that feed upon each other to create a negative self-fulfilling prophecy.

To earn your living by doing what you love, you will face a constant stream of challenges and barriers. Finding out how to get yourself into the zone and to be there as often as possible will help you achieve what you want to achieve.

I hate everything except my shoes

To show you how, I'm going to take you far away from the world of sport. I'm going to introduce you to someone who for many years lived a frustrated and sometimes unhappy life because she ignored her intuition. When you are often in the zone you become highly intuitive and use it to supplement your physical and mental strengths.

Sandra Deeble took a long time to find this out. When eventually she did, it led her to a life that she had imagined, just as van Nistelrooy had visualized his goal. Unlike him, though, her goal wasn't clear for a long time and as he says, 'sometimes, if you are not so confident, you stop'.

She stopped many times. One Christmas some years ago, she returned from London to live with her parents in Hertfordshire. She had the happy knack of landing one job after another, each one – to the outside observer at least – higher paid and better than the last. Yet each time something was wrong. None of these jobs felt right. She didn't feel right physically, emotionally or intuitively.

She found herself in debt, living with her parents at the age of 32, and still not knowing what she wanted to do. Just knowing that what she had done before was not right for her.

Maybe she should have listened to her inner eight-year-old sooner than she did.

I found a letter in the loft in my parents' house in one of these shoeboxes that people keep full of birthday cards and things like that from when they are little. There was a letter that I got from *Twinkle* comic.

It said: 'Dear Sandra, Thank you very much for your short story, which we like but unfortunately we can't use.' I just couldn't believe it. I couldn't believe that at that age I was motivated enough to write a story, type it and get it in the post.

When I was eight, I remember getting a toy typewriter. A Lilliput. There was the Petite and the Lilliput. The Petite had lots of TV advertising and was plastic. I wanted the Lilliput because it was metal and just seemed more professional.

Her parents must have encouraged her; after all, someone posted the letter to *Twinkle* comic. Yet Sandra recalls that a series of mental blocks built up that stopped her from thinking like an eight-year-old. Her father, like many others, was concerned that she should keep her feet on the ground

I think that was all seen as play. My dad was very much, 'Make sure that when you get a job you get a good job.' We had to choose A Level subjects. I said I didn't know what subjects I wanted to do. He said, 'Well you just don't know what you want to do full stop.' I said, 'I do, actually, I'd just love to live in the country and write books.'

He said the classic thing. 'There are very few people in this world who can do that', he said – that was a dream. He also said, 'If you had any talent for writing it would have shown through by now.'

Despite her 'dream', Sandra spent many years acting out her father's words: 'you just don't know what you want to do full stop.'

I was a bit clueless about the world of work. I just followed what I was good at, so I did a French degree. I remember a careers talk, when somebody came and described TEFL [Teaching English as a Foreign Language] and all I remember from the talk was she said 'I sit on the balcony with a brandy and I watch the sun go down', and I thought, that sounds good to me.

So I went to Spain for two years, which I loved and just thought I would carry on teaching English and travel round the world. Then I realized that I actually missed England. Friends and family, and stuff like that.

I came back. Again, completely clueless about what I could do. Just trying to find anything, really. That seemed to be the aim – to get a job. So I thought that if I do a secretarial course, I could go to different types of industries and work my way around to see what I liked doing – which, looking back, would have taken the rest of my life. So I ended up working as the PA to the marketing manager in a packaging company. I did quite enjoy it because this man allowed me to do bits of his job, and part of that was getting involved in design, which I really liked.

But she was restless. She knew she should be doing something, but wasn't sure what it was.

Then I saw an ad in *The Guardian* one day, a very small ad and very non-specific. It just said something like 'Are you tenacious, creative and able to hit the ground running?'

It turned out to be this very high-profile industrial design consultancy in Islington. They wanted someone to do PR, marketing and profile-raising activities. Somehow I talked my way into it. At the time I didn't really understand or know what product design was.

I was in that job for a couple of years. They just let me get on with it and do things that I thought of. I was quite good at new business, getting through the door. All the designers dreamt of the clients they wanted to do work for, but were too scared to pick up the phone, whereas I just didn't care. Also, I didn't take rejection personally.

So that was an easy thing for me to do. From time to time I would think, 'I didn't choose this.' But because I was young and living in London, it was quite exciting and glamorous.

There then followed a series of moves that could have been scenes from a film called *How to Succeed in Business Without Really Trying*:

I don't know how this happened, but before I knew it I was at some recruitment consultancy that specialized in design, going in for another job in design. Then I ended up working for a very high-profile retail branding consultancy called Fitch. I remember I thought I'd really arrived, because everyone had heard of it.

There I was the Head of New Business, which was a bit of a joke, but they had obviously heard that I was good at it. I remember the first day someone saying, 'We are hoping Sandra will bring in a few million pounds of new business in the first six months.'

She laughs out loud as she recalls keeping a straight face as they outlined their expectations.

I just started doing ridiculous things like getting telephone directories for Latin America, because she knew I spoke Spanish and said that would be a good market to get into. So I would just sit at my desk, phoning department stores in Argentina and Chile, trying to get meetings. The people at the other end of the phone were so astonished that this girl was calling from London to ask to meet them.

When it came to someone saying to me, 'Do you think it's worth two of us flying out there?', I just really didn't think it was, and I don't think I could have coped with the plane journey knowing that at the other end the person I'd arranged a meeting with had forgotten and gone to lunch.

I did lots of things like that. I remember calling Tetra Pak, and the marketing director said 'Yes, I'll meet you.' So two of us flew to Sweden, and of course it was embarrassing because when we got there they said he'd gone out to lunch. The man had completely forgotten. Because to him it's just was something to fit in his day, whereas for us it was a big thing.

I did get some new business because fortunately, I worked with people who were good at selling. I was the 'get in the door' person and they were able to convert – which was a big word at Fitch, 'conversion'.

I remember I had this feeling every day of not living authentically. I remember socially as well people saying 'We've heard about your job, you've just come back from Sweden or Barcelona', and I just remember thinking, it's not really me.

I felt really troubled by it, and I always felt a kind of unrest as if there was something else that I should be doing, but I had no idea what that was.

Shortly after I had started this job, people were constantly saying 'We're really glad to have you as part of the team, and it's really good to have you on board and what are you going to be doing?' I really didn't have a clue. I was just making it up as I went along.

Then something simple happened. Something that, in time, incredibly was to change the course of her whole life – she got a corn on her foot.

I remember getting a corn on my toe, to the point where it was really painful to walk. Somebody recommended me to this foot person, who's quite glamorous and has been on daytime telly, called Michael Keet. He runs the School of Reflexology in London in Covent Garden. I went along to see him and he said, 'Oh yes, I can fix it, no problem, but you've got to look at why you have got a corn.' I asked what he meant and he said, 'You are obviously not balanced in the way you are walking – you're putting pressure on one side of your body and you weren't doing that before. What's going on in your life?' I said, 'I've just started this new job. I just feel I can't handle the pressure. Everyone's expecting so much of me. It doesn't feel real. I feel as if I am acting every day, and one day I'm going to get found out and they will realize I can't really do it.'

So he said 'You've got to look at your life and look at the balance. Whether you are doing what you really want to do. In the short term, go and get yourself a pair of Birkenstocks, because they will realign your body' – which I did.

It was before Birkenstocks were really, really trendy. I remember wearing these to work and they called me Fred Flintstone. Everyone was wearing Patrick Cox shoes and I was wearing Birkenstocks. Of course, people in all design consultancies wear them now.

This man said 'I can sort your feet, but what about your life? You don't look too good. For someone of your age, you're not radiant.' On the way home, I just burst out crying. It was just that thing where a perfect stranger had seen that all was not well. It seemed strange that during the day, everyone thought I was doing brilliantly.

Just by looking at her feet, the reflexologist could see that Sandra was fighting an internal battle. She knew it too, but it seemed that she was on a merry-go-round that just would not stop turning.

You would think at that point I would have sorted myself, but again I was headhunted by another design consultancy and found myself going for another round of interviews.

I just thought, 'What on earth am I doing?' Again, I think it was that I had no idea. Friends would ask what I would do if I wasn't doing what I was and I just did not know.

That was a big part of the problem. It's all very well to give up what you are doing, but you have to know what else it is that you want to do. All I knew was that I didn't want to be doing that. I couldn't really visualize another kind of life.

I remember once bringing a laptop home from work to write a proposal. I was sitting at the kitchen table mid-morning and I thought it was absolutely fantastic. I said to my friend, 'I had the most amazing day – I was just pottering around, sitting in the kitchen, and the sun was coming through on the kitchen table and I was just free to do what I wanted when I wanted. Wouldn't it be great if that's how I worked?' He said, 'But what would you actually be doing?'

I didn't have a clue. I remember that day I had a kind of insight into how it might feel to be doing something, but I didn't know what that might be. So then I find myself at another design consultancy. And really, at that point I'd lost the plot completely.

It was another promotion with a different kind of job. I was Senior Project Manager. It suddenly made my previous job seem like a holiday camp. It was so rigorous and they did corporate identity, and I was constantly being asked to scope projects and I just didn't know what people were talking about.

It's a weird thing when you can be there in meetings and part of it, and I just thought I had a kind of defect in my brain, I couldn't understand this language that they were talking, and people were asking things like 'Could you go off and do a brand audit?' Everyone around you just assumes that you know what to do, so rather than say that you don't know, you think you'll just go along with it until they find that I can't.

They didn't. Everyone was delighted that I was on board.

I remember getting two new suits from Nicole Farhi so that I looked the part. I think that was 90% of the challenge. If you look right, people don't question you.

That's when my turning point was. I'd been in the job for a month. There was this pressure building up and I just knew that it was the wrong thing.

———

For Sandra Deeble, this was crunch time. As she felt the pressure building she increasingly felt unauthentic: almost as if she were a fraud.

It was a lot to do with the environment – it felt so unauthentic. I was sitting at my desk and I just thought 'I've got to leave, I've got to get out of this building now.'

I really just wanted to leave the building, but I thought I ought to tell someone I was going first. So I worked with this woman, my line manager. I said 'I've got to tell you I really think I've made a terrible mistake by coming here.'

She immediately thought, because I'd been doing scoping, that I meant budgets. She asked 'Is it something to do with the figures?' I said 'No – I shouldn't have made the decision to come here.'

Then I had to see the man who headhunted me and he immediately said 'You've got another job.' I said 'No, I haven't – I just know that I need to leave now.'

He asked if I knew what I wanted to do. I said, 'I don't know what I want to do, but all I know is that I don't want to do this. If I carry on working in this environment, with the pressure, I'm never going to have the space in my head to think about what I might do.' It was quite a funny thing. So many people came up to me and said, 'You're so brave.' Loads of people made *Star Trek* references about 'to boldly go'.

This woman said 'It's only the very bold who dare to leave something because they know it's not right, even though they don't know what they are going to do.'

I was giving it up for nothing.

———

That Christmas, she turned up at her parents' house for the holiday. When they asked how long she could stay for, she replied 'Probably for a while'. She then explained how she had left her job and given up her flat.

Now, you would think that this would be the moment. The moment when Sandra Deeble found her destiny. It wasn't quite that simple.

They couldn't believe it. I was an only child in what they thought was a glamorous job in London and I'd come home to roost to be in my child-hood bedroom.

I hadn't planned it, so I had debt. Not huge debt, but ongoing credit cards and things like that. In London I had a salary and now I didn't. I thought, 'I really need to earn some money', so I went to a temping agency, and you know when you just think 'How stupid'.

Although people kept saying I was brave, I think a lot of the time they were thinking I was just stupid.

I had to do things like a spelling test and I did a typing speed test and I don't think I came up to scratch on either. I didn't think I was employable. As soon as I got home my mother shouted, 'The agency's called – they've got something for you'.

It was a job at the head office of Tesco. She began the very next day. She must have looked somewhat out of sorts unpacking stationery and tidying up the stationery cupboard in her Nicole Farhi suit. Then the merry-go-round started to turn again.

After a few weeks, the Head of Design had noticed she looked different.

This man wandered over and asked what I was doing there. I told him I was temping. He said 'No, what's someone like you doing in a place like this? I can tell you don't normally do this.'

He said, 'I head up the design team. Why don't you come and free-lance for us?' On the one hand it was great because my earnings went up. But here I am again doing what I had been doing, but not what I had chosen at all.

So still living with her parents, and freelancing in the Tesco design team, she was feeling a little better. At least leaving the job in London meant she was being half honest with herself. Yet here she was, back on the merry-go-round – precisely where she didn't want to be. Then one afternoon she let her intuition kick in, and something quite remarkable happened.

It was 4 pm and it was that lull when everyone goes to the chiller ma-chines to get Kit-Kats and things to boost their energy, and try and make the time go more quickly. I just remember looking round about me, and it was just that office scene, which just doesn't do it for me, and all those grey carpets and those boards that divide people, and I just thought: 'What am I doing? Here I am again doing what I don't want to do and I still don't know what it is I really want to do.'

I don't know what it was, I just suddenly got this chemical reaction in my body, and I felt that something was leading me that wasn't a 'head thing' at all. I just walked over to my computer and sat down.

A friend of mine had said 'If you don't know what you want to do, you just have to focus on what you love.' I remember saying that there was absolutely nothing that I loved. He said 'What's really good in your life? Even things that you own?' I said absolutely nothing. I said the only thing I liked was my Birkenstocks.

I felt happy and grounded when I was wearing them. They used to make me feel good and they were quite quirky, they used to make me laugh and they were always a talking point. People would ask me about them.

He said, 'Focus on your shoes.'

So that moment in the Tesco head office I sat down and I just suddenly found myself, and it wasn't conscious, I found my fingers literally doing the walking and typing 'Why I love my Birkenstocks'. It took me about twenty minutes or so to write this piece, but I wasn't thinking 'I am writing a piece', I was just literally expressing myself. I just remember feeling – for the first time in years – totally in the moment. My body was relaxed and the time just flew.

It was like being in a trance really. I sort of came out of it and realized that I had written an article, and again it wasn't a conscious thing, it was just not planned. Before I knew it I had picked up the phone to this magazine and said that I had written this thing – it was *Marketing Magazine* and they had a column called Design Choice – I asked if they had ever had shoes as the design choice. I faxed it over and they published it.

It was just the most amazing thing. It went into print and it was only afterwards that I thought, 'Oh my God. Some people actually earn their living just from doing that.'

This revelation sowed a seed in her mind, and she began writing in secret. She bought herself a laptop, and when friends asked why, she said it was so that she could type her freelancer invoices at home. Slowly, gradually, she began to inch her way towards a life that she could love. She just began to make chance opportunities.

I started writing in secret. Not having a clue about how to get published in newspapers, and I would just write things for fun. Just choose a subject, and write things, and the only people I showed were my parents.

Then one day I thought I would just have a go. I called *The Independent on Sunday*, and they said something like 'Send it through', so I used to fax it. I probably did about half a dozen features on no subject that had any kind of 'news hook' whatsoever. Never heard anything, didn't even know about following it up, didn't know anything.

Then one day I just got a phone call from the Features Editor. She said, 'I just have to say that I have been getting the stuff that you've been sending, but we'll never, ever be able to use it'. I was so excited. 'Why's that?' I asked. She said 'Because we don't know who you are. And that's not the way you go about it.' I asked what to do, and she said 'The normal thing is that you send us an idea and if we like it, we would commission it. But we wouldn't commission you anyway, because we don't know who you are – so who are you, then?' I said 'I'm just trying to write for myself at home and I've never actually done this before.'

She said 'It's a very sure style, you wouldn't know that you've just started writing.' I asked what to do and she said 'You can send me some ideas but I really don't think we'll be able to use your stuff because you're not a known writer.' So that was it. That night I just did ten ideas and put them in the post.

Next day she called me. She said 'We want to commission one of your ideas.' It was unbelievable … I'll never forget that rush, it was just so exciting.

I did this thing that was called 'I'll just show Paul his room'. It was Christmas time and I was going out with a man who lived in Australia, and he was coming over to stay in England. I was still living with my parents and my mum wanted to put him in a separate room. I asked friends, and everyone – people who were living with their partners – said they went home for Christmas and were put in separate bedrooms. Isn't it a joke?

So I did this thing about young people being separated in their parents' homes. It was eventually published in *The Independent on Sunday* in the Real Life section, just between Christmas and New Year. It was the most exciting thing ever and I got £100 and that was it.

Elated, Sandra wanted more of this, yet friends and family were quick to reintroduce doubts about the idea of writing full time.

I said it would be so fantastic to be able to do that full time, and someone said 'Yes, but it's not as though you're a journalist or anything, is it?' It was as if she was saying that was just a one-off, she thought I was just lucky.

Another friend said there are very few people in this world who are able to earn their living doing what they love. It's only the lucky few. I thought it may be just the lucky few, but I'm going to be one of those lucky few. It made me really angry that she could accept that the majority of the population had to accept doing something they didn't love.

I was so determined at that point.

And so, just as Ruud van Nistelrooy had sat in his hotel room and begun to play the match over in his mind, Sandra Deeble now had a goal and began to play her destiny over in her mind. She continued with her freelance work, got a mortgage and moved out of her parents' house.

I started to write during the evenings and at weekends and then gradually, as I started to get published, I dropped all my other work. I remember one year I did four days a week, then three, then two. Then in January 2000, I just gave up all my other work and thought 'It's now or never.'

I remember that the first six months of that year were a nightmare. I woke up on January 1 and thought 'Well now I'm going to write full time', and of course it took weeks to get the first commission because everyone was saying 'Oh, we are fine for January'.

I was following my heart regardless.

After all those years of struggling with her feelings of something not being right, she has at last understood what it is like to have that feeling of elation and control which athletes refer to as being in the zone.

It's all been about intuition, which is why I find it so hard to advise other people. They say what did you do, and I say well it was just literally following this feeling. It was all about how I felt – in my body as well.

The more I've done it, the more aware I've become of my body, so the minute something becomes wrong I sort of feel it.

The last proper posh design job I had, I felt uncomfortable in my body – not just physically, but not right. The out-of-balance thing. It just felt so fake. Then when I was writing, it just felt so natural, like being myself really.

I do believe. I've got this card above my desk that I've had for years: 'Do what you love and the money will follow'. I've had so many times when people have said 'Well at least you tried it, you could always go back to what you did before.' But you know it just makes you so determined not to.

For me, it's as much about lifestyle as it is about writing. It's that feeling of waking up every day, never questioning whether I'm doing the right thing. And I have had opportunities over the last few years to do other things. Maybe I'm a bit stupid, but I'm always pulled in this other direction.

She's achieved the dream that she had as a young girl: as well as writing for quality newspapers and magazines, she has a regular column My Workspace in *The Guardian*, has authored five books for lifestyle publisher Ryland, Peters & Small, and is writing her first novel.

It's interesting that all of this has been achieved without any journalistic qualification and without a business plan. It was all about a struggle to find out what she really loved – something that I believe had been locked in her subconscious since childhood. It was all about creating chance opportunities, thinking like an eight-year-old and creating her own belief system: once she believed she was a writer and developed the tenacity to make it happen, she became a writer. It was all about creating a sticky ball and building connections, and finding her way into the zone.

It feels self-indulgent sometimes. I just think, 'How the hell have I got away with it?'

It does distress me when I see people who are living a lie, who are in denial really. Who just can't leap, for whatever reason. It is fear. For a lot of people it is that not wanting to give up the material. They are just so cushioned by things like bonuses.

Sandra Deeble has realized her dream. It has been a struggle: a struggle between heart and head; a struggle against other people's perceptions of what is possible; and a struggle against the expectations and constraints that adults can place upon children, and that we can place upon ourselves.

When she found out what it was that she loved, she 'leapt before she looked' – something that you may say is foolhardy, but when you are in the zone, you feel in control to the point where you don't stop to think.

Does van Nistelrooy slouch?

Watch any athlete at the peak of their powers. There is something about the way they move, the way they hold themselves. When Ruud van Nistelrooy is on song, you don't see him slouch.

Getting your body feeling just right is part of the key to getting in the zone. Researchers have shown that our body posture actually affects the way we feel, not just that, our feelings affect our posture. Working with patients suffering from clinical depression revealed that they adopt an almost imperceptible stoop, leaning forward ever so slightly as they walk. Controlled trials showed that teaching patients to walk straighter had an impact upon their mental well-being.

You may not be able to hone yourself into a world-class athlete, but it stands to reason, if you are to take on a major challenge and earn your living by doing what you love, you will have to look after your body as well as your mind.

Many athletes can report having been in the zone but are at a loss to explain how or why they got there. Often, being in the zone is associated with a lack of memory; a distortion of time. Sandra Deeble talks of entering a trance-like state when she wrote her first article: she said that the time just flew by. Athletes in high-intensity sports often describe the state as 'dreamlike' and say they feel as though time is slowing down.

Psychologists are agreed that there is no one single method that will get you into the zone: how you do it will depend very much on whether you are an artist or an athlete, an illustrator or an illusionist.

Yet they do tend to agree that it is a state in which you are acting without thought, you are totally connected to your performance – flowing rather than processing.

If we could all be in the zone all of the time, we would. All sorts of internal and external factors contribute to make up how we are feeling on any particular day. Sometimes we are up and sometimes we are down.

It is important to take control of the way you feel so that, regardless of the circumstances, you are up more times than you are down, and that you feel the intensity and elation of being in the zone as often as you can.

Check and decide

It is nobody's responsibility but our own to get ourselves into that state called the zone. We can all develop our own intuitive zone-meter, to assess where we are at any particular point in time, and decide where we actually want to be. We can exercise control over our feelings. We can, if we want to, change state in an instant.

Imagine a scale of 1 to 10. At level 1 we are at our lowest ebb. Around levels 4–6, we are feeling okay, but not particularly moving towards something that we care for. In the levels 7–9, we are operating at a high level of performance – even peak performance. On the occasions when we can reach level 10, we are in that elusive state called the zone, when we are flowing and it almost feels as if something has taken us over: as with the 'trance-like' state described by Sandra Deeble.

The key to controlling how you feel and your level of performance is to first of all check out where you are on the scale and then decide where you want to be.

It is no good saying, 'I can't help the way I feel, it's because of this and because of that.' You *can* help the way you feel. The way you feel is related to the way you think. This is very important, because your behaviour is not related just to your ability, but to the state you are in at this moment.

There are two good ways to change your state. First of all, change the way you use your body – does van Nistelrooy slouch?

Just improving your posture, even a little, will help you feel better. Develop patterns of movement that create confidence in you and give you a sense of strength, flexibility and fun.

Eight years after having her corn treated by a reflexologist, Sandra Deeble went back to see him. It was he, remember, who told her that her posture had caused her foot problems and that she should look at her life. She describes their meeting.

> I went back to see him last year, after eight years. He didn't recognize me immediately but I said that I'd come back to thank him and I told him the story. Then he remembered it. He said, 'You looked as if you were hiding yourself away – you were all scrunched up. Now you look fantastic: your spirit is leading you now.'

She found a way into the zone and it showed physically.

The second way is to change your focus. In the way that lucky people turn bad luck into good, you can change the way you feel just by changing your focus of attention.

I remember asking a seminar group to write down five things that made them feel good. I suggested that they could focus upon these to change their state from bad to good instantly. One lady in particular looked sceptical about such an idea and huffed and puffed her way towards making a list.

I asked her first how she had got on. She replied 'Not very well, but I have managed to make a list.' So I asked her to pick something from the list that made her feel good. She grimaced a little and looked down her list.

Then she began to describe the image of her little children snuggled up in bed fast asleep and how it felt to see them safe and secure. I could not have picked a better person. As she did this, her face truly beamed, her eyes widened and became moist, her shoulders lifted, her body relaxed and she looked as if she was happy to be alive.

She had gone from huffing and puffing sceptic to a picture of pride and happiness. I asked how long it took to change her state. She replied 'an instant'.

That is all it takes, if we set our minds to it, if we focus, if we take personal responsibility for the way we feel. We can change state in an instant. In a blink.

Blink into the zone

There is more than just one way to raise your state. It is important to develop a whole raft of possibilities, because what may work one day may not work the next. Don't try to analyze it – just accept it.

I began by listing 20 things that make me feel good. Over time I have added to it so that I now have a long list of things that I can try when my state isn't at the level I need to accomplish what I want to achieve.

When you don't feel that you are in the right state, you must do whatever it takes to change your state. To some, this may feel like self-indulgence. For example, my list includes walking in the forest, sitting by a fire, reading a newspaper and drinking great coffee. Imagine a winter afternoon that combined all of these: it sounds like a holiday. Yet I know that it can be time well invested. If it gets me into the right state to apply massive sustained effort to achieve what I have to achieve, then I know that I can do great things. And so can you.

So before you begin to write down the first 20 things that make you feel good, here are a few of the ways that Sandra Deeble blinks into the zone:

Get inspiration

Read inspiring stories about people doing what you would most like to do. Whilst suffering a sticky patch when she was writing her novel, she began to read other authors' websites. Suddenly the words started flowing again.

Cook

Sandra says: 'Cooking really does it for me. If I get stuck or feel niggly, I make a cake or something chocolatey. Chocolate mousse or something really yummy. Also things like risotto are fab: slow and soothing. I think cooking is a great mood enhancer. You've also got something to show for your efforts rather than staring at a blank page.'

Dig in

In the summer, she has been known to go outside and start digging and planting. She says 'Something about the rhythm of doing something physical and being creative in a different way really helps. I also think that it relaxes your mind: before you know it, an idea has come to you and you want to get back to the words. Gardening and cooking are sometimes better than walking, where you can focus too much on what's not flowing, it's harder to lose yourself in it.

Bathe

She will often have a bath in the middle of the day and end up getting out to scribble something down.

Be good to yourself

'I think the other thing is to be kind to yourself. It's very destructive to keep telling yourself that you're useless and a time-waster. Sometimes, when things are really not flowing, I'll just go out for the afternoon – to bookshops or to a café, I've got a few favourites where the hot chocolate is very good!'

Afternoon movie

Go to the cinema or be like Sandra Deeble and watch a black and white film on television. She says: 'You come back feeling recharged – it's fantastic. Julia Cameron calls this "filling the well", very important, I think, particularly if you work on your own. You have to keep topping up your creativity, otherwise it goes. You need to put back and find new inspiration.'

In conclusion

What makes changing your state so great is that you get to do and think about things that you like, and when you change states, you are better equipped to achieve your goals.

I think we are conditioned, if we are struggling with our work, to simply grind out a result. Sometimes needs must, but most times we can create the time and space to change our state and perform better. Often it requires very little time at all – just a focus and a blink.

I like to preface my changing state work with a quotation taken from Anthony Robbins' book, *Awaken the Giant Within*:

You are alive – you can feel good for no reason at all.

That's good, because to do what you love, you have to make sure that you can feel good and work at peak performance a lot. Before you know it you will find yourself in the zone – in a blink.

9

Change your world – how small things make a big difference

Magic Boomerang was an Australian television series that began in the late 1960s. It featured a young boy Tom Tumbleton, a sheep farmer's son, with an amazing secret: his magic boomerang.

When he threw the boomerang, time stood still. His little world stopped, giving him just enough time to change the course of history, to right a wrong or to enhance someone's life. It was a small thing that made a big difference.

At around the same time, the golden couple of Australian television, Michael Maurice Harvey, Musical Director with ABC, and Penny Spence, Australia's first female news reader, did a small thing that in time was to make a big difference. They conceived a daughter, Eugenie.

Now Eugenie Harvey is the charismatic driving force behind a new movement *We Are What We Do*, which published *Change the World for a Fiver – 50 Actions to Change the World and Make You Feel Good*.

Published on a shoestring, the book has become a worldwide phenomenon, selling 100,000 copies in its first three months and spawning a Channel Four series of short animation films. It is about to be published throughout the world.

In creating the book, she has given each of us a 'magic boomerang'. We have a chance to stop the world for a moment and make some small changes. Small things that make a big difference.

Amazingly, she had to reach 'rock bottom' before she put her energies into what she loved, and it was a small thing that made all the difference to her life.

Change the World for a Fiver is an amazing little book. It looks like it could have cost £15 to produce, yet it retails for exactly £5. Over 100 people helped to create the actions and images. They are all really simple. Many of them make you laugh. None of them cost anything to do. Yet they do make a difference. A few of my favourites are:

- **Action No. 1: Decline plastic bags whenever possible.** Every person in the country uses an average of 134 plastic bags every year – that's 8 billion bags all together. A plastic bag can take up to 500 years to decay in a landfill. There is an alternative: it's called a shopping bag, and apparently in France it's very chic.
- **Action No. 11: Get fitter, feel better.** Obesity is turning into a massive problem in the developed world. One suggestion by doctors is to do something simple, such as walking up a couple of flights of stairs every day. Although if you are obese, you are inevitably not going to want to do this because it will make you sweat a lot – which will draw attention to the very thing you're trying to deal with. So much for doctors! But try walking as much as you can. If that's only from the dessert trolley to the cheese board – that's a starter. Well, no, it isn't – it's a pudding. But you get the idea.
- **Action No. 35: Write to someone who inspired you (postcard provided).** Nice to do. Nice to get. What is there not to like about it?

And so it goes on. Improving relationships with your neighbours; caring for the environment; being kind to strangers; experiencing things that you have forgotten about; showing appreciation.

All small things, but they can change your immediate world. If enough people do them, they can change our world.

The story starts on the other side of the world. A talented lady from a talented family always thought she was destined to do something special or important, but she really struggled to find out what it might be.

I think it was a natural assumption that I had, that I would do something one day that would be something I'd feel very proud of, would be of a scale, and possibly, a bit out of the ordinary.

I just had this feeling as long as I can remember. I've always had a feeling in the pit of my stomach that I would do something really interesting one day.

Growing up, she was surrounded by interesting and successful people. – not least her parents:

I have two parents who are both very successful in their careers. They did, I suppose, slightly unusual things. My dad's a musician and was the musical director of the biggest TV station in Australia for 35 years. My mum was an on-air presenter. She was the first woman to read the news on Australian television – ever.

Neither of her parent's professions appealed to her. Eugenie knew that she didn't have any real musical ability and, having seen the television industry from the inside, it had little appeal for her. She knew that she loved theatre and for a time toyed with the idea of becoming an actress. She began her working life in the theatre, though not treading the boards.

I wanted to be an actress for a little while. I got a job working down at the New Theatre Company and I think that was the first thing, the first step on the journey to achieving what I wanted to do. In that first job, I was given my first break by a chap called Michael Lynch, who ran the Sydney Theatre Company then, which is our equivalent of the National Theatre.

Michael went on to run The Sydney Opera House and he now runs the South Bank Centre in London.

If you don't quite know what you want to do, put yourself in an environment that makes you happy. I didn't quite know if I could be an actress or not. I didn't quite know what I could do, but I loved the theatre and I loved the performing arts. I got a job in the box office selling tickets, and then a job became available when I got my degree as the receptionist. That's when I went and asked Michael, 'Can I be the receptionist?' He said, 'You've just got a university degree, you'll stick at it for ten minutes.'

But he gave me a go and I was on reception. Then a job came up in the press office, and I just grabbed it and became the publicist, then the head of PR, and then I did some communications roles there for about five years. It was a small company and I got the opportunity to really make my mark. Without any real design I was on the way to having a career in public relations. In a sense that was something of a red herring, because I didn't really want to work in public relations.

Nevertheless, she seemed to be good at it. She wondered if she was really good, or if she had just found herself in a friendly environment where people wanted to be nice to her.

I think I wanted to test myself, to see if I was actually any good at PR or if it was just that I was working in an arts organization where I had a natural affinity to that, and perhaps people were just being kind to me.

I saw a job advertised for a company called Foxtel, which is Rupert Murdoch's pay television company, our equivalent of Sky. It was Corporate PR Manager and it was probably twice the salary I was on. I didn't think I had a hope in hell of getting it, but I went for it and I got it in a blink – in a heartbeat, really.

It was quite a shock, but I was also incredibly flattered and I thought, 'This will do me.' It was television and my parents had been in TV, so I thought maybe that would be a good thing to do.

So I threw myself into an environment that was utterly terrifying to me and I felt very poorly equipped. Perhaps that was another step along the way. I perceived myself as being in over my head and quite terrified, but just having to make a go of it. And of course that was a really good thing. I was there for three years and did do really well, but I found out that PR was not for me. I don't want this to sound arrogant, but I had the misfortune to be very good at something I didn't like.

It has been a bit of a cross around my neck in some ways. When you are good at something and people keep giving you more money to do it, you keep on doing it, but it was making me very unhappy.

I didn't like doing it but it was appropriate. The skills I used to do it are the skills that I use to do the work that I now do – communication, writing, collaboration, good relationships and networking. Those are the skills that I'm very proud of and enjoy using.

What I didn't enjoy was the application of those skills. Essentially, what you are doing in PR is promoting another product or another person's talents … you're constantly getting on the phone, blowing somebody else's trumpet. This was all part of the process that was going on in the back of my brain. I was starting to think that I had ideas and things to say. I'd spent eight years getting on the phone saying have I told you about this actress or this playwright or this producer or this new TV show or this new policy that we are putting through in the pay TV industry. You know, brokering information effectively. I was starting to think, and get more confidence in my own ideas.

Eugenie left Foxtel as a success, and with the confidence to re-invent herself. Thanks to her father (who is English), she held a British passport and headed off to London with a germ of an idea in the back of her mind.

The next thing I thought I might do was to be a stand-up comedian. When I was younger I was quite a funny girl, I was good at presentation, I was very good at speaking, and I have a way of looking at the world. My dad was a very funny person and I was very curious. I certainly wasn't going to try out being a stand-up comedian in Australia, where it's a small pool. I wasn't prepared to fail in it, and I certainly wasn't brave enough to reinvent my career in Australia. So I thought I'd go to the UK, where I didn't know anyone, and use my anonymity to see what I could become.

Her plans were thrown off a little almost immediately when she realised that to live in London was horrendously expensive. She had sold her car in Australia, and the money from that and her savings went little further than a deposit on a flat and a travelcard. She needed to make some money fast, so she took a job in PR. Although PR was not where she wanted to be, it led to her 'ker-ching' moment.

Unbelievably, I got a job doing PR for the Australian Tourist Commission in the two years up to the Sydney Olympic Games. There I was, doing PR. Really, really miserable, but at least I was working out that if I had to do PR or do something that I didn't like, at least I had to have some integrity.

I could see no integrity with respect to Murdoch in pay TV. But to be saying that Australia's a great country and you'll have a great time if you go there, there was an integrity and honesty and authenticity in me saying that.

I had travelled extensively in Australia and I was very passionate about the country and the people. I think that was a 'ker-ching' moment.

You have them but at the time you don't register them – or I certainly didn't – as being ker-ching moments. But that was one for me. Working on something that you believe in that has an integrity is something that I enjoy and was important to me.

But what about stand-up comedy? Did she have what it takes to make it behind the mike? She helped out on a voluntary basis at a comedy club and went on a stand-up comedy course. Then she got a chance.

I got a couple of gigs in try-out nights. At the very first one I knew within about 30 seconds of standing up there that there was absolutely no way that I was ever going to be a stand-up comedian. It was the most exhilarating and fantastic thing.

So that's another thing that I would say to people, if they have a monkey on their back. I thought for a long time that I would be very funny, I assumed it, and I absolutely wasn't. It was a relief because then I could think, 'Well, that didn't work – what's the next thing?'

She went back to Australia at a low ebb and her mother encouraged her to give London another try. She did and – you guessed it – ended up working in PR again. When she finally hit 'rock bottom' she did what lucky people do – she turned bad luck into good.

My sister had just had her second baby in Australia and I was at this really, really low point and she rang me. Literally minutes after she had given birth, and I was in my little studio flat. It was a very sad, tragic time. I just heard this happiness and I had never, ever heard such happiness in my life. I hung up and I felt really, really blue for a minute – I was obviously really happy for her, but sorry for myself.

I just had this absolute epiphany. I had this thing. All of a sudden I realized – because I didn't have children, huge financial commitments or a relationship – that I didn't have anyone depending upon me, and I just thought that the world was my oyster. It's a classic example of looking at exactly the same set of circumstances from the other side of the table.

I just realized that I had total liberty. I also realized it wouldn't always be like that and that one day I would have commitments and just couldn't do whatever I wanted.

That was a really big moment.

Whilst grinding away at PR for a finance house, the staff were given a presentation by David Robinson, the founder of Community Links, an East End charity. Eugenie realized that her skills could be applied to do simple things, small things, which would make a big difference to people living in poverty, and had a flash of inspiration.

At the time I was thinking about how I could do something with a social purpose, and starting to have the confidence to say 'I want to make the world a better place.' Which is quite a thing to say.

I started to be bold and say that I wanted to change the world and be part of social change. I found my voice and I found my passion and I met the person who enabled me to express that. We had absolutely nothing. I went out there and talked to David and we said 'Let's give it a go.'

I quit my job and I moved to a friend's place where I didn't have to pay rent and I lived on my savings for three or four months. In this, time the seeds of the idea for the movement 'We Are What We Do' were sown.

We worked at our idea and talked to a few people, and then Lord Joffey gave us £25,000. That paid us both to work on it for the first year, and after two years of development, going round seeing hundreds and hundreds of people, creating projects and initiatives to bring our ideas to life, we launched on September 30, 2004.

The flagship project was the publication of *Change the World for a Fiver*. They had set themselves a target of eventually selling 10,000 copies. After just six weeks it began to appear on the bestsellers list, and by Christmas 100,000 copies had been sold, and all on a shoestring budget. But of course, it's not just about selling books.

Our ambition with my project We Are What We Do is to make a very real difference to the world. It's been very, very successful. I don't look out of the window and think that the world has changed – and I don't know if that will ever be something I'll necessarily see out of the window.

I would like to feel that I was part of moving something on. I don't think it will ever be one thing or one person or one project. The stakes are high in terms of where we are at in the world. I think we either have the choice to be the generation that stuffed the world up, or the generation that saved the world, and I hope that I will feel that I was part of the latter.

All of the profits from the project go back to the charity, Community Links. Eugenie no longer has to live on 'the whiff of an oily rag', as they are inundated with requests for commercial spin-offs.

She had hit rock bottom and simply changed the way she looked at her life. She is creating an initiative that allows us all to do the same. She earns her living by doing something that she loves.

Ever since she was a girl growing up in Australia she has had a feeling in 'the pit of her stomach' that she would do something interesting or special. Maybe this is it – or maybe it is just the start. Either way, it is showing the way, how small things can make a big difference.

Magic boomerangs, blinks and sticky balls

By now, if you have come this far in the book, you may be thinking that this is all so simple.

I hope that you are, because it is. The essence of earning your living by doing what you love is combining a whole series of small things. Not just any old small things, though: those small things that really can make a big difference.

The 'magic boomerang' effect of *Change the World for a Fiver* gives a series of actions that, on the face of it, look as though they can have no impact at all. For me, they have helped enhance the relationships that I have with my children, my friends and my neighbours. Professor Ruut Veenhoven of Rotterdam's Erasmus University has spent the past 20 years examining human happiness. His analysis suggests that we can improve our overall happiness by up to 15% simply by improving our intimate relationships. Small thing, big difference.

Changing our state from low to peak performance can happen in a blink. When we are at our best, we achieve more. Small thing, big difference.

Creating compelling stories and connecting with the right people can make ideas grow and 'tip' just as epidemics do. No big advertising budgets, no massive mailshots, no double-glazing-salesman-on-speed behaviour. Just small things making a big difference.

And so it is with creating visualizations of what we want, developing our luck or accentuating our millionaire mind. I'm not suggesting that you do anything massive here, or anything that I am not doing myself.

Now. This is the moment. The moment when you must start to think about your future, your happiness and what you are going to do to get them.

It is the moment when you will have to decide whether you can get your courage to spill out over the table.

10

Aha, ker-ching

Over the years I have come across a lot of people who are avid readers of self-development books – so much so that they can critique them all. They develop almost a cynicism that there can be nothing new.

In that sense, they may well be right. Perhaps there is nothing new – only different ways of combining ideas and producing different results in different settings.

What disturbs me is when I see an avid collector of these books who may have become a credible critic and is living the same old life. Doing the same old thing. Looking for some Holy Grail that will lift him or her to a new plane. Worst of all, sneering cynically when others try things.

They have the answers in their hands. They develop paralysis by analysis. They have so many techniques broken down in so many ways that they don't know which way to turn – so they buy another book.

Stop analyzing – start thinking. Less is more. You don't need more information, you need greater insight.

If you can develop this insight, use small things that make a big difference and find your own courage, you too can earn your living by doing what you love. But you must act.

I have proven it to be true. So has a man who sells 'waking dreams'; a musician who hates the music business; an irreverent reverend; a inner-city hard man who wants a better life for kids; a merchant banker who gets paid in passion; an adventurer who thinks like an eight-year-old; a writer that found her zone late in life; and a charismatic Australian who has a simple goal – to change the world.

They are ordinary people, just like you and I.

They have chosen to live extraordinary lives. So can you.

Tune in to your instincts

It's comforting to have lots of analysis, plans and projections, but they can also frighten the life out of you. They can also constrain what you believe is possible.

That's a shame, because they are all invented. We like to think that more information will give us more certainty and security; often, it just makes us more confused and frightened.

Our instincts are highly sensitive instruments. They can make instantaneous assessments of situations with not very much information at all. Many of us have forgotten how to listen. Start to tune into your instincts more each day. Look back every so often to see when you were right to listen, and when you were off-beam. All of the people featured in this book put instincts before analysis and they are all doing what they love.

Perhaps there is something in it.

Do things that have integrity

You will be happier and more successful if you can do things and behave in a way that gives you a high degree of integrity. Eugenie Harvey, although unhappy in PR, felt more comfortable with it when she was working on showcasing Australia as a destination in the run-up to the Olympics.

She could believe in the message that Australia is a great place to go to. She felt she was acting with integrity and honesty. She realized that having integrity in your work is a key element in doing what you love.

Many people do work that goes against their personal value systems if the money is good. I believe that if you go against your values and beliefs, it can actually be bad for your health. Sandra Deeble found this: she was on a merry-go-round of one 'good' job after another, yet it was making her ill. Her reflexologist described her as 'scrunched up'. She describes how she felt that she was 'acting' every day and that one day she would get found out. Before she was found out, she followed her instincts and discovered how to put integrity into her life.

You must be clear of what your values and beliefs are. If you have never enunciated them, write them out. Take responsibility for being the guardian of your own integrity. It is nobody else's fault if you go against your values and beliefs.

Must you wait for your epiphany?

Many people have their 'aha' experience or their 'ker-ching' moment when they are at their lowest ebb – I should know, it happened to me. Sandra Deeble, Eugenie Harvey and Gerry Epstein have all described an epiphanic experience when at a low ebb.

In one sense, moving from your lowest ebb could be seen as being useful. When you feel you have reached rock bottom, where else is there to go but up? However, it is quite dangerous to wait until you feel absolutely sunk and drained. You are operating from a vulnerable position – a position of fear.

In his book *The Empty Raincoat* Charles Handy describes the sigmoid curve as a way of looking at how we can reinvent ourselves. It is a curve that, if we place it on a graph, represents our life-cycle (see Figure 10.1).

Figure 10.1 *The life-cycle curve*

At the bottom of the curve, we come into existence with a big bang. The curve dips a bit at first as we get used to the confusion and the noise of this new world. Then we begin the journey upwards. We are nourished and get strong; we begin to toddle and then to walk; we go to school; finish our education; and get a job. We peak, retire, slow down and then die.

In previous generations, this life-cycle would have stretched out for 70 or 80 years. Most people would have had a job for life. Today, you are lucky if your job lasts five years before you do something else. Most of us will have to begin many new curves during our working lives (see Figure 10.2).

Figure 10.2 *Starting a new job*

When you begin a new curve at point B, you are on the way down: you are sinking and all the variables are going against you. It is a position of fear. It is hard to create a new curve from here. But you have to.

According to Handy, it is better to begin a new curve when you are at point A. Not surprisingly, this is difficult because all the signals that you are receiving are that you are on the up – everything is fine. If you leave it too much longer, though, you will find yourself heading towards a position of fear.

Have your 'aha' moment, your 'ker-ching' moment, your ephiphany. But do you have to leave it until the last moment?

New space brings new people

There is comfort in the familiar. If you are not doing what you love now, and you want to re-invent yourself, then you must learn to let go of the old and create the new.

Gerry Epstein was a psychoanalyst and psychiatrist steeped in the Freudian tradition, supported by a significant income. When he began to develop 'waking dream' therapy, he had no-one to turn to. He was ostracized by his profession. He said something that I know to be true from my own experience.

Other people started taking notice of me. When you do this, and make a space, new people come into your life. As you discard your old paradigms and belief systems, new people start to enter into your existence.

When you set off to do what you love, don't cling to the past because it is comfortable. Define and create your own space. A space that new people want to enter into.

Have faith and your beliefs will become your reality

Successful writer Sandra Deeble changed her life. She did not suddenly gain an infinitely better grasp of the English language or punctuation, or improve her power of metaphor. One thing changed, and it changed everything else: her belief. She began to believe that she could write quite well. This belief changed her focus. Her lucky behaviours and her determination became directed and focused towards writing. As she focused, things began to happen. She created a new space and new people came into it, and today, she is Sandra Deeble – 'writer'.

She is actually Sandra Deeble – 'person with new beliefs'. There are no diplomas or degrees to lend support to the notion that she is a writer. She just had to change her belief and that, in turn, affected her actions.

She took a leap of faith, just as most of the people in this book did. When I asked Gerry Epstein why he gave up his successful psychiatric practice to do something that nobody in New York had ever heard of, he didn't even pause for thought. 'Faith', he said.

You are what you believe you are. Have faith.

Micro is the new macro

Andrew Mawson helped to create a sticky ball that began to transform the nature of run-down Bromley by Bow. He did it by understanding the detail of people's everyday lives. He says that the answers to the big questions, the macro, can be found in the micro.

Gerry Epstein helps people transform their lives and deal with physical and mental conditions. He does it not by enmeshing people in drawn-out therapies and analyses related to macro theories but by creating visualizations. A micro input to produce a macro output.

How do you change the world? Set up Earth Summits and rely on politicians? It would be nice to think so – these are macro reactions. According to Eugenie Harvey, 'We are what we do.' Everyone can take some small actions to make the world a better place. The micro is the clue to the macro.

When you start to do what you love, try to remember this. Grand strategies and plans can be very grand, but what works is what counts.

Money follows ideas

Every single person in this book set off and created something out of nothing. They gave life to an idea and by using the sticky ball principle and the power of connections, they attracted money towards them.

Money doesn't follow any old ideas though: you have to work at your good ideas. This can be great fun, because all you have to do is learn to think like an eight-year-old. People who think like eight-year-olds have amazing ideas. They decide to change the world; they walk to both poles; they create food concepts that accountants can't understand; they become journalists without any qualifications; they put a nursery, a dance school and an art gallery in a church.

The people featured in this book have shown that these things can really happen, and that people will put money towards ideas that are really 'out there' if you do the right things.

Your idea may seem crazy, but you have to treat it as though it is perfectly normal, according to Robert Swan, the polar explorer:

> No matter how stupid or crazy the idea might be, you have to treat that idea in a very normal way. Not play on it. There's nothing I hate more when people come to me now with a crazy idea and say to me, 'It's such a crazy idea. Aren't I something different and special to have such a crazy idea?' I tell them to bugger off.
>
> If they come to me with an idea and they say 'We want to try and do this, this and this', then I'm listening.

> I try to have 100 ideas a week. Ninety-nine of them may be rubbish. My most important job is to figure out which 99.

Whatever you do, keep having ideas. You can never have enough ideas, because money follows ideas.

Make your own luck

According to Sandra Deeble's father, 'Only the lucky few can earn their living by doing what they love.'

I think he added one word too many there. You do have to be lucky, but why should luck just apply to a few people? Luck is not finite. It doesn't run out if too many people are having it. We can create more and more good fortune for ourselves if we apply the principles of luck. We can be amongst the lucky many. When we create a belief, we adjust our focus. We are in a fantastic position when we:

- focus our lucky behaviours on doing what we love;
- create sticky balls;
- build rich connections;
- apply our millionaire mind;
- think like an eight-year-old;
- get in the zone; and
- realize that small things can make a big difference.

We are lucky people because now we have all that it takes to earn a living by doing what we love. If you have reached this far in *Bear Hunt*, you are a lucky person indeed, because you now know that there is only one thing stopping you.

It is you.

You have a choice. You can do what you love.

Notes and references

Chapter 2

- *The Human Mind: And How to Make the Most of It*, Robert Winston, Bantam Press, 2004.
- *Now, Discover Your Strengths*, Marcus Buckingham and Donald O. Clifton, Simon & Schuster, 2004.
- More information about Gavin Cargill and his organisation can be found at www.valuetheperson.com.

Chapter 3

- *Waking Dream Therapy*, Dr Gerald Epstein, ACMI Press, 1992.
- *Healing Visualizations: Creating Health Through Imagery*, Dr Gerald Epstein, Bantam New Age, 1989.
- For a full list of Dr Epstein's publications, go to www.kabbalahoflight. com.

Chapter 4

- For more information about the Bromley by Bow Healthy Living Centre, go to www.bbbc.org.uk.
- Andrew Mawson is now President of Community Action Network, a support network for social entrepreneurs. Full details can be found at www.can-online.org.uk.
- *We're Going on a Bear Hunt*, Michael Rosen and Helen Oxenbury, Walker Books, 1997.

- *The Tipping Point*, Malcolm Gladwell, Abacus, 2002.
- 'We shall go on to the end ...': speech reproduced with permission of Curtis Brown Ltd, London on behalf of the Estate of Sir Winston Churchill. Copyright Winston S. Churchill.
- *Living on Thin Air: The New Economy*, Charles Leadbeater, Penguin, 2000.

Chapter 5

- Phillip Collins is now the Director of the Social Market Foundation. For information, go to www.smf.co.uk.
- *The Luck Factor*, Richard Wiseman, Century, 2004.

Chapter 6

- To find out more details of the Personal Enterprise Profile (PEP) questionnaire, see www.humanfactors.co.uk.

Chapter 7

- Robert Swan is the founder of Mission Antarctica and continues to lead expeditions of business people, educators and young people to clean up Antarctica. For details, see www.missionantarctica.com.
- *A Whack on the Side of the Head*, Roger Von Oech, Warner, 1998.

Chapter 8

- Sandra Deeble's column 'My Workspace' appears every Saturday in *The Guardian*'s Jobs & Money section.
- *Awaken the Giant Within*, Anthony Robbins, Pocket Books, 2004.

Chapter 9

- *Change the World for a Fiver*, Short Books, 2004.
- To help change the world in your own way, go to www.wearewhatwedo.org.uk.

Chapter 10

- *The Empty Raincoat: Making Sense of the Future*, Charles Handy, Hutchinson, 1994.

Index

Aboulker-Muscat, Collete 28, 30, 67, 72
Ah-ha moments *see* ker-ching moments
Antarctica 106–7
Arsenal 121–2
Atkinson, Dr Adrian 77–9, 81, 86–7, 95, 101

Bannatyne, Duncan 81
Bearhunt 50–2
beliefs 3, 32–4, 35, 40, 49, 140, 150
Bell, Santiago 37, 42–4, 49
Berscheld, Dr Ellen 18
Blakebrough, Eric 39
Bromley by Bow 50, 67, 73, 150
   Healthy Living Centre 47–8
   move to 40–2
   transformation of 43–8
Brown, Gordon 61, 64

Cameron, Julia 137
Cargill, Gavin 18–21, 68, 74
Change the World for a Fiver 139–40, 145, 146
choice 1, 10
Churchill, Winston 52, 54
Collins, Phillip 7, 69
   enthusiasm for new job 63–4
   making his own luck 64, 65
   positive attitude 64–5
   resigns from job 61–3
communication 19–21
Community Action Network (CAN) 48
Community Links 145
commuters 8
connections
   building 59
   making 42–9, 51–2, 151

power of 55–8
creative thinking 103–4, 107–9
   don't get trapped by the rules 110–12
      be an explorer 116–17
      believe you are creative 118
      challenge rule/pattern 111–12
      decide what can be discarded 112
      laugh 112–13
      looking foolish 113–14
      switching off your logic button 114–16
      take some risks 117–18
   fight for the right to be wrong 109–10
   having fun 110

Davis, Greg
   change of direction 92–3, 98
   door security business 92, 96–7
   feeling of separateness 94–5
   food project 95
   turning bad situations into good 96
   UEW project 93–4, 98–100
   upbringing 94
Deeble, Sandra 5–6, 123, 148, 150
   aimlessness of 123–6
   becomes a writer 130–2
   being in the zone 132–4
   turning points 126–30
dormant enterprisers 9

earning a living
   dissatisfaction with 1–2
   doing what you love 2–3
   formula for 3–4
   personal experience 4–5
Edstone Hall 77

eight-year-old thinking 103–4, 107, 108–9, 118–19, 123, 133, 151
enterprisers 82–3, 89
entrepreneurs
  attitude to personal risk 82, 83–4
  background experiences 80
  characteristics 81–2, 89–90
  feeling of separateness 94–5
  gender differences 79, 85–6, 87–8
  luck and tenacity 85
  recognising 77–9
  scratching that itch 100–1
  social 91–100
  stick to the knitting 80–1, 84–5
Epstein, Dr Gerald 5, 35, 150, 151
  application of mental imagery technique 28–32, 33
  as conventional physician, psychiatrist, psychologist 25–6
  creating new beliefs 49
  epiphany 27–8, 71–2, 149
  meets his mentor 26–7, 67
  ostracized by colleagues 29, 73

failure 20, 85, 117–18
faith 31–2
fear 149
Ferrer, Paulo 42
Fisher, Helen 17
the formula
  case studies 5–7, 9–10
  common themes 10
  discovering 3
  do things that have integrity 148
  great people doing great things 5
  have faith and beliefs will become reality 150
  ingredients 4
  make your own luck 65–76, 152
  micro is the new macro 42, 43, 150–1
  money follows ideas 50, 151
  new space brings new people 150
  tune in to your instincts 148
  waiting for your epiphany 148–9
Fox, Sue 45, 49
Freud, Sigmund 27, 72

Gallup Organisation 21
gap-year students 8
Giggs, Ryan 122
Gladwell, Malcolm 55–6
  Law of the Few 55, 56–7
Good, Eve 43–4, 49–50

Handy, Charles 149
happiness 2, 3, 4, 88, 146, 148
Harvey, Eugenie 6–7, 139, 148, 151
  belief in doing something special 140
  hits rock bottom 144
  idea into practice 145
  ker-ching moments 143, 144–5
  succesful work experience 141–3
  upbringing 141
Harvey, Michael Maurice 139
Hodge, Margaret 61, 64
holidays 1
Hucknall, Mick 11
Human Factors International 87

imagery see mental imagery
imagination 109, 114–16
insights 147
instincts 148
integrity 148
intuition 70–2, 135

jinx theory 75
job satisfaction 84
Jowell, Tessa 45
Joyce, Chris 7, 11, 66, 71, 73
  see also Love Saves the Day

ker-ching moments 27–8, 41–2, 63, 71–2, 129–30, 148–9
King, Martin Luther 35, 52

Leadbeater, Charles 50
let go of the old/create the new 150
love 2
  attachment 18
  attraction 17–18
  irrational 18
  knowledge concerning 16
  lust 17
  pink lens effect 18
Love Saves The Day 71, 73
  background 11–13
  establishing the business 14–15
  origin of name 13
  philosophy behind 15–16
  reactions to 13–14
luck 146
  being consistent 75
  bouncebackability 74
  creating 66–7
  cultivating 64, 65
  making your own 152

principles 65, 66
    boost your intuition 71–2
    build/maintain strong network 67–8
    don't dwell/take constructive steps 75
    expect good fortune 72–4
    expect interactions with others to be
        lucky 74
    get lucky 75–6
    have a relaxed attitude towards life 68–9
    ill fortune will in the long run work out
        for the best 74
    listen to your lucky hunches 70–2
    maximise your chance opportunities
        66–70
    open yourself to new experiences 69–70
    perseverance and tenacity 72–4
    turn bad luck into good 74–6, 85, 97, 101
    recognising 65–6
    self-fulfilling 118

magic boomerang effect 139, 146
Manchester United 121–2
Mawhinney, Dr Brian 47, 73
Mawson, Andrew 5, 37, 67, 68, 69–70, 71, 73,
        150–1
    makes connections 42–9
    moves to Bromley by Bow 40–2
    telecommunications training 38
    trains to be clergyman 39
mental imagery 5, 49–50, 72
    application of 28, 36
    background 25–7
    having a dream 34–5
    insight into 27–8
    preparing the mind
        changing 34
        cleansing 34
        intention 33
        quieting 33–4
    revisiting images 25
    right-brain thinking 34
    successful 33
    way of the imaginal 28, 29, 35–6
    what you believe you create 30–2, 33, 72
mid-life crisis/success 9
Millennium Dome 115
millionaire mind 80, 86–7
    create own environment 90–1
    developing 91
    social entrereneur 91–2
    types 88
        corporate 89
        enterpriser 89

entrepreneur 89–90
    technical and professional 89
motivation 20–1, 88
Mums 8

National Health Service (NHS) 110–11
National Lottery 117

passion 61, 64
Personal Enterprise Profile (PEP) 78, 86–7, 88
Pie In the Sky café 45, 49
Pinochet, Augusto 37
public sector workers 8
Puttnam, David 112

Reid, John 45
relationships 42, 59, 68, 146
right answer culture 109–10, 118
risk management 75
Robbins, Anthony 138
Robinson, David 144–5
rules, challenging 45, 112–18

Scott, Captain Robert Falcon 104, 105–6
silver surfers 8
Simply Red 7, 11
Social Market Foundation 63
Spence, Penny 139
sticky ball 23, 38, 59, 146, 151
    Bromley by Bow example 42–9
    creation of mental images 49–50
    diffusion process 55–8
    going on a bear hunt 50–2
    and women 51–2
storytelling 52–3, 74, 146
    giving it oomph 53
        be prepared to play different roles 53
        be succinct 53
        blood, toil, tears and sweat 55
        don't be personal 54
        emphasize emotional content 53
        everyone loves a good story 54
        have a point 54
        re-experience the event 53
        use descriptinve sensory language 53
        vary your vocal style 53
    relating to 53
StrengthsFinder 21–3
stress–related illness 1
Sunday Evening Syndrome 1
Swan, Robert 6, 151
    living his dream 103–7
    losing/regaining focus 107

talent
innate 21, 23
recognising 18–21, 23
themes 22–3
connectedness 23
futuristic 22
ideation 22
relator 22
strategic 22
Taylor, Michael 39

underachievers 8
unemployed 8
United Estates of Wythenshawe (UEW) 93–4,
98–100

van Nistelrooy, Ruud 121–2, 132, 134
Van Oech, Roger 107–8, 118
Veenhoven, Ruut 146
Viles, Jean 45–6
visualization 121, 123, 132, 146

waking dream 27, 36, 67, 150

We Are What We Do 139, 145
what works is what counts 39
Winston, Robert 16
Wiseman, Richard 66, 68, 70, 71, 73
word-of-mouth
Connectors 57
Mavens 58
Persuaders 58

Zander, Benjamin 118
Zendo 26
the zone
blinking into 136
afternoon movie 137
bathe 137
be good to yourself 137
cook 137
dig in 137
get inspiration 136
change your focus 135–6, 139
check and decide 134–6
getting into 121–2, 134
take personal responsibility 136